PERESLAVL-ZALESSKY
ROSTOV (VELIKY)
BORISOGLEBSKY
NIKOLA-ULEIMA
UGLICH
TUTAYEV
YAROSLAVL
KOSTROMA
KRASNOYE-ON-THE-VOLGA
PLIOS
SUZDAL
BOGOLIUBOVO
VLADIMIR
YURYEV-POLSKY
ALEXANDROV
ZAGORSK

THE GOLDEN RING

AURORA ART PUBLISHERS · LENINGRAD

Text by Fiodor Kudriavtsev
Translated from the Russian by Galina Strelkova
Photographs by Irene Stin and Anatoly Firsov
Designed by Klara Vysotskaya and Victor Levchenko

© Aurora Art Publishers, Leningrad, 1976, 1988
Printed and bound in Yugoslavia

3 $\dfrac{4902020000\text{-}650}{023\,(01)\text{-}88}$ без объявления

ISBN-5-7300-0144-4

The "Golden Ring" is the name of a tourist route popular with both Soviet and foreign lovers of old Russian architecture. The route, winding in and out of cities and villages in the north-eastern part of what used to be the State of Muscovy, is hardly circular, but it certainly is "golden" in the sense that it is rich in historical relics and towns that are museums in themselves. These man-made "stone records" of the past have witnessed historical events, the suffering and heroism of the nation. Each of the sixteen sections of this book is devoted to the most remarkable places of historical and cultural interest.

Fifty years ago many splendid specimens of medieval architecture were in nearly total neglect. It is due only to the enormous efforts of Soviet experts that the buildings have been restored to their former beauty and elegance. It is particularly gratifying to know that not only well-known scholars, architects, archaeologists and historians took part in the work but that they were frequently assisted by local people – civic leaders, teachers and specialists in regional lore – who appreciated the unique value of these treasures. Many contemporary figures will appear in our accounts of the monuments of the Golden Ring.

The scope of restoration work expanded considerably after the end of World War II. In 1966, the government of the Russian Federation set up the All-Russia Association for the Preservation of Historical and Cultural Monuments, and it is this organization which conceived the idea of making the Golden Ring a special sightseeing route.

The tour begins and ends in Moscow with excursions in the Moscow, Yaroslavl, Kostroma and Vladimir regions. As soon as we leave Moscow and get on the Golden Ring route, monuments of the past come into view. Off to the side, near the road to Yaroslavl, there are Pushkino, Bratovshchina, Rakhmanovo, Muranovo and Abramtsevo, as well as Safarino, Vozdvizhenskoye and the earthen ramparts of old Radonezh. The contours of the Trinity-Sergius Monastery in Zagorsk appear on the horizon like a vision from the past. We could begin our tour from there, but let's keep it in chronological order, and start with the much older town of Pereslavl-Zalessky, the birthplace of the Russian Prince Alexander Nevsky. Legend has it that he built a summer residence on the outskirts of Pereslavl-Zalessky. The site, known as Alexander's Hill, is still shown to the tourist. We shall come back to Zagorsk later, so now our first stop will be on the shore of Lake Pleshcheyevo, behind the high earthen ramparts of Pereslavl-Zalessky.

GLOSSARY

boyar: the upper stratum of feudal society in Russia (10th–17th centuries), possessed of many exclusive privileges until their partial abolition by Peter the Great

caftan: an ankle-length coatlike garment

druzhina: a prince's personal troop of soldiers

kokoshnik: a purely decorative architectural feature; semicircular in shape, often rising to a point (like the traditional Russian head-dress of the same name) and framed by a moulding

kremlin: an inner fortress or citadel of the reigning prince

oprichniki: specially chosen corps of life-guards of Ivan IV (the Terrible)

posad: town's trading and artisan quarters

refectory-type (trapeznaya) church: the main square-shaped building of the church itself adjoined on the west by a low refectory linking it with the bell-tower

sloboda: a settlement near big cities in feudal Russia whose inhabitants were temporarily exempt from taxes and other duties

veche: town council made up of the people's representatives or people's assembly, which usually met in the main market-place

zakomara: the semicircular upper section of the outer wall, covering the adjoining cylindrical inner vault and reflecting its shape

PERESLAVL-ZALESSKY

Pereslavl is one of the most ancient cities in Russia. In the tenth and eleventh centuries it was a fortified Slav settlement called Kleshchin. The ancient ramparts can still be seen from across the lake. Yury Dolgoruky is considered the founder of Pereslavl-Zalessky. His rule was a difficult one for ancient Russia. Her strongholds in the south toppled one after another. Hostile nomads from the plains preyed on the Slav tillers of the soil. Gradually the inhabitants were forced to retreat into the north-eastern regions beyond the dense, virtually impenetrable woods (*Zalesye*). They arrived there by round-about river routes and gave the rivers and new settlements Russian names in memory of the homelands.

They named one of the settlements Pereslavl-Zalessky after the old town of Pereslavl on the Trubezh River in the Kievan State. And the winding river on which the new town stood they named the Trubezh. The river flows into a lake which they called Pleshcheyevo.

When Prince Yury Dolgoruky decided that the site of Kleshchin was unsuitable, he had the settlement transferred to the southern bank of the Trubezh. For protection he ordered a moat dug, and earth ramparts and a stockade put up. He had a castle for himself and cottages for his men built. In 1152, he laid the foundation of the white-stone Cathedral of the Transfiguration of Our Saviour. Yury Dolgoruky did not live to see the work completed by his son Andrei Bogoliubsky.

The white cathedral stands on Red Square beyond the kremlin ramparts which are still steep, as they were in ancient times. It has stood there for 800 years, the oldest architectural monument of the Russian north-east, including Moscow. In its austerity it resembles the churches of Novgorod. Each of the external walls is decorated with semicircular *zakomaras*, the middle one a bit higher than the others. The curve of the apses is ornamented with a simple frieze, a line of vertically set stone and little arches. On the drum carrying the dome there is also a "skittle" border reminiscent of the wooden tiles hewn of aspen wood. With the passing of time the building seems to have sunk into the ground. It appears smaller, but is still stately and beautiful. In front of the church there is a statue of Alexander Nevsky inaugurated in the 1950s.

Aside from the cathedral, few of the other kremlin buildings have survived. The oldest of them is the Church of the Metropolitan Peter which dates back to 1585. It was probably modelled on the famous Church of the Ascension in the village of Kolomenskoye (now within the city limits of Moscow). It has the same cruciform plan, the same open galleries above an arcade, and the same faceted tent-shaped roof on an octagonal support. The onion-shaped dome rests on a small drum with a decorative band around it.

Pereslavl-Zalessky is proud of its three monasteries which add so much to its beauty. The oldest of them is the Goritsky Monastery said to have been founded during the reign of Prince Ivan Kalita.

The entrance to the monastery with the tiny gate-church and the gate-keeper's lodge alongside is a remarkable example of seventeenth-century architecture. The plan of the church is asymmetrical as are the outer walls, which are richly adorned with carving and tiling. The "casket studded with precious stones", as the church was called a hundred years ago, still attracts the attention of archaeologists and architects as a rare surviving specimen of medieval art.

Worthy of notice is the large seven-domed Cathedral of the Dormition dated 1757. In the interior the splendid painting and white stuccowork on a light blue background recall the ornamentation of the Cathedral of the Resurrection at the Novo-Yerusalimsky (New Jerusalem) Monastery in Istra, on the outskirts of Moscow. The resemblance is not surprising since the iconostases in both cathedrals were designed by the same architect, Karl Blank, and executed by the same team of craftsmen headed by Alexei Petrov.

The Danilov Monastery is situated in the low, south-western end of town. Commissioned by Prince Vasily III, the single-domed Cathedral of the Trinity was built in 1530–32 in honour of the birth of Vasily's son Ivan, who was to go down in history as Tsar Ivan the Terrible. The Abbot Daniel was put in charge of the construction.

This shrewd monk not only managed to rise to a high position, but succeeded in getting himself so into the good graces of Vasily as to stand sponsor at Ivan's christening. In its exquisite simplicity and perfect proportions the cathedral is comparable to the ancient Cathedral of the Transfiguration of Our Saviour. It looks festive and imposing even without much ornamentation. Only an unusually gifted person could have conceived it. This was probably the "stone mason" architect Grigory Borisov, whose name will come up a number of times on our Golden Ring tour. In the latter half of the seventeenth century the renowned Gury Nikitin and his team of artists decorated the walls and vaults of the cathedral. The frescoes are of the greatest artistic value; particularly impressive is the Saviour.

Next to the Cathedral of the Trinity there is another single-domed building, the Church of All Saints. Small, pleasant and cheerful-looking, it was built in 1687 by Prince Bariatinsky who later became Brother Ephraim of the Danilov Monastery. A stone memorial plaque in the south wall marks his burial place. The surrounds of two adjacent windows are gaily ornamented with different designs. The unknown architect must have been a light-hearted fellow who wished to leave an imprint of his happy nature in stone. The belfry nearby was built only two years later, but evidently by a different architect judging by the heavy tent-shaped roof and square base.

Only two secular buildings have survived at the Danilov Monastery – the Refectory and the 200-foot long Dormitory.

Although there are several more seventeenth- and eighteenth-century buildings left in the town that are worthy of our attention – the Church of Our Saviour and St Cornelius (1696–1705), for example – the St Nicetas Monastery on the road to Yaroslavl is far more interesting.

Building was an unhurried process in old Russia. Sometimes it took decades. Lime for construction purposes was seasoned for three or four years. Bricks were moulded, baked and dried slowly at kilns set up near the building site. But the St Nicetas Monastery was completed in just three years (1561–64). Tsar Ivan the Terrible intended to convert the humble monastery into a stronghold for himself and his *oprichniki*, but changed his mind at the last moment in favour of Alexandrova Sloboda.

In 1608, the St Nicetas Fort-Monastery withstood a two-week siege by Jan Sapieha's Polish invasion force. It was badly damaged by fire, but was restored in 1643. A little church erected in the time of Vasily III is the oldest building of the St Nicetas Monastery. Although it is now a chapel of the five-domed cathedral designed by the architects of Ivan the Terrible, it has retained the original trifoliate design of the rounded *zakomaras*, adding interest to the somewhat mediocre architectural plan of the larger building. Some of the designers possibly came from the Caucasus together with the Kabardinian Princess Maria Temriukovna, who became the Tsar's second wife. That would account for the eastern influence evident in the lancet arches supporting the drum of the central dome, an unusual feature for Russian architecture.

The spacious refectory-type Church of the Annunciation with its beautiful silhouette and superb architectural details belongs entirely to the middle of the seventeenth century.

Supplementing the ensemble is the rather heavy turret-like tented bell-tower, with the wall and its towers providing an excellent example of sixteenth-century fortification.

Another high, tiered bell-tower dating from 1818 stands at the entrance to the monastery. At one time it was considered "an alien body". But this criticism is unjustified. The bell-tower fits in well with the ensemble, its clear-cut vertical lines heightening the architectural effect. Without it the St Nicetas Monastery ensemble would appear lower and flatter.

1. *Pereslavl-Zalessky. View from the Goritsky Monastery →*

2. *Pereslavl-Zalessky. The Cathedral of the Transfiguration of Our Saviour. 1152–57*

3. *Pereslavl-Zalessky. The Monastery of St Nicetas. 16th–19th centuries*

4. *Pereslavl-Zalessky. The Church of the Metropolitan Peter. 1585.*
   Gallery. 18th century. Bell-tower. 19th century

5. *Pereslavl-Zalessky. Tent-shaped roof of the Church of the Metropolitan*
   Peter. 1585

6. *Pereslavl-Zalessky. Goritsky Monastery. 17th–18th centuries →*

8. *Pereslavl-Zalessky. Goritsky Monastery. Decorative detail of the entrance gates. 17th century*

9. *Pereslavl-Zalessky. Goritsky Monastery. The Church of All Saints and the Cathedral of the Dormition →*

11. *Pereslavl-Zalessky. Danilov Monastery. 16th–17th centuries*

12. *Environs of Pereslavl-Zalessky →*

ROSTOV (VELIKY)

In old Russia only two towns were called *veliky* (great). One was Novgorod, the other Rostov (now Rostov Yaroslavsky) which has stood on the shore of Lake Nero for eleven centuries. Even before the coming of the Slavs it was a big fortified settlement inhabited by local tribes.

The flourishing, commercial town of Rostov was governed by a *veche*. The population accepted the rule of princes with reluctance. They felt even more inimical to the Christian faith which was being imposed on them. In fact, Bishop Leonty was killed for his overzealous efforts in introducing the new religion, and it was seventy years before the ecclesiastical authorities thought it safe to ordain a new bishop. Only Prince Andrei Bogoliubsky, known for his harsh methods, succeeded in subduing the unruly inhabitants but even he hesitated to make his home in Rostov, the finest and largest town in his principality. In 1162 Prince Andrei erected the white-stone Cathedral of the Dormition. Since then it has been re-built a number of times, but the original foundation, the lower part of the walls and fragments of the twelfth-century frescoes have survived.

As we travel on the road from Moscow, a panorama of rare beauty unfolds before our eyes some seven miles out of Rostov.

Across the lake there is an enchanting view of the silvery domes of the Cathedral of the Dormition, the white-stone walls of the kremlin, the Monastery of Our Saviour and St James, and in the distance the very old St Barlaam Monastery. Just before entering town we see the lovely little Church of St John the Divine. Standing on the bank of the now shallow Ishna River, it is the last of the wooden churches in the Yaroslavl region.

Today Rostov offers the visitor a look at its kremlin and Metropolitan's Residence. The latter, with its silver and gold cupolas and towers, cornices and crosses of lace-like design, resembles a castle out of a fairy-tale. But it is only lately that we have been able to gaze at all this splendour. In 1953, a tornado struck the town uprooting trees and carrying off the roofs of houses. The domes of all the churches were swept away leaving the buildings grossly deformed. The reconstruction of Rostov is one of the most brilliant achievements of Soviet architecture.

Most of the kremlin buildings were erected in the late seventeenth century over a period of only 15–20 years by the Metropolitan Jonah of Rostov, who had the funds for such a project; his diocese was one of the wealthiest in the country and he could afford to hire the very best decorators and stone cutters.

The eleven-tower kremlin wall built by the Metropolitan extended for about $\frac{2}{3}$ of a mile, but it had little military significance. It was not a proper fortress such as were constructed late in the seventeenth century.

Originally the stone buildings of the kremlin included the Chambers for Church Dignitaries, the Royal Chambers, and the Metropolitan's Residence. Later additions were four churches and the Red, White, and Otdatochnaya Chambers (where people came to pay their respects). Subsequently the Metropolitan's Residence was reconstructed and a number of passageways installed.

The Church of the Resurrection above the main entrance to the monastery was the first to be built (1670). Standing on a high substructure opposite the Cathedral of the Dormition, it is crowned by five domes and decorated with the ogee *zakomaras* characteristic of the Metropolitan Jonah's time, which form the 24 slopes of the roof. Similar in design and even more graceful is the Church of St John the Divine (1683) at the west wall. Flanking each of the two buildings are round towers with cube-like scaled roofs made of aspen tiles which are relatively durable and very attractive. When aspen is exposed to the air, it acquires a silvery hue and a silken sheen.

The Church of Our-Saviour-over-the-Entrance-hall with a single golden dome is the house chapel of the Metropolitan's Residence. The exterior is modest – a double-hipped roof, a band of arcading, and barely discernible pilasters. But inside it is more luxurious than the other churches. Only a third of the area is assigned to the congregation. The *solium* is on a higher level, with eight steps leading up to it. Overhead there is an arcade supported by gilt pillars with pendants between the arches. The altar is on a still higher level with a stone barrier for an iconostasis. The frescoes decorating the walls are of local workmanship, and the chandelier and candelabra are from the Metropolitan Jonah's time.

The Churches of the Resurrection and St John the Divine also have a stone wall instead of the more usual wooden iconostasis. The *solium* at the Church of the Resurrection is half as high as the one in the Church of Our-Saviour-over-the-Entrance-hall. The *solium* at the Church of St John the Divine is quite low. It was considered "unseemly" for the Metropolitan to stand higher than his distinguished guests residing at the adjacent Red Chambers. The frescoes in both churches were executed by Gury Nikitin and Sila Savin of Kostroma and Dmitry Plekhanov of Pereslavl-Zalessky.

The Cathedral of St Gregory of Nyssa is situated outside the kremlin enclosure. It occupies the site of the old St Gregory Monastery where in 1214 the first educational institution in the Russian north-east was founded.

The recently restored White Chambers and the Red Chambers (practically raised from ruins) harmoniously supplement the kremlin ensemble. Such old secular buildings are all too rare on the Golden Ring. The old way out of the kremlin lies underneath the Church of the Resurrection, beyond which there is a square where the *veche* once gathered and where the majestic Cathedral of the Dormition with its famous bell-tower stands.

Next to the kremlin we find the Church of Our Saviour-on-the-Market where remarkable seventeenth-century frescoes are now being cleaned. In the town itself is the St Isidore Church built in the time of Ivan the Terrible. The structure, which had been disfigured due to inept reconstruction, now appears in its original aspect.

One of the oldest architectural ensembles, St. Barlaam's Monastery, occupies the site where a temple to Veles, the god of farm animals, once stood. Other buildings of interest are a later Monastery of Our Saviour and St James, with another "Jonah-type" church; and the Church of Our Saviour-on-the-Sands (all that has survived of a monastery founded by Princess Maria, widow of the Prince Vasilko of Rostov who was tortured to death by the Mongols in 1238). Princess Maria has the distinction of being the first and possibly the only woman chronicler of events in medieval Russia.

The names of other remarkable women of Rostov appear in the annals of Russian history. Princess Darya Rostovskaya and Princess Puzhbolskaya donned suits of armour and fought valiantly on Kulikovo battlefield in 1380. Irina Lugovskaya emulated their example in the seventeenth century. She later became the wife of Count Musin-Pushkin. She was known in London and Amsterdam as a scholar. Foreigners deemed it an honour to meet her. Indeed, in her younger days, she would have become the wife of Tsar Alexei had it not been for her father's "low" birth. Widowed at an early age, she made Rostov her residence, collected old books and chronicles, and helped the Metropolitan Jonah in the construction of the kremlin.

The learned noblewoman presented the decorators with the *Theatrum biblicum* by Visscher Piscator. Today we recognize some of its illustrations in the frescoes of Rostov's churches. Irina Musina-Pushkina died at an early age, but not before she had inculcated her son with her own passion for Russian history. Ivan Alexeyevich continued to add to the family library, which became part of the celebrated collection of his grandson Alexander, the most famous member of the literary Musin-Pushkin family, descendants of the remarkable woman who lived in Rostov Veliky 300 years ago.

13. *Rostov (Veliky). The kremlin. 16th–17th centuries →*

14. *Rostov (Veliky). View of the kremlin and Cathedral Square ⇒*

15. *Rostov (Veliky). The kremlin. View from the Water Tower ⇒*

16. *Rostov (Veliky). The kremlin. Belfry. 1682–87*

17. *Rostov (Veliky). The kremlin. Belfry. 1682–87. Bells*

18. *Rostov (Veliky). The kremlin. The Church of St Gregory of Nyssa.*
    C. 1670 →

19. *Rostov (Veliky). The Church of St John the Divine. 1683. View from*
    the wall passageways →

20. *Rostov (Veliky). Domes, tented towers and chimneys. Latter half of the 17th century*

ЗАВИСТЬ
ИНЕНАВИСТЬ

24. *Rostov (Veliky). The Church of Our-Saviour-over-the-Entrance-hall.*
1675. Fresco

25. *Rostov (Veliky). The Church of the Resurrection. 1670. Fresco*

27. *Rostov (Veliky). The kremlin. Red Chambers. 1670–80*

28. *The Church of St John the Divine-on-the-Ishna, near Rostov (Veliky). 1687–89 →*

BORISOGLEBSKY

The road north-west from Rostov Yaroslavsky to Uglich and Lake Beloye lies mostly across forested areas, and it was for the protection of travellers that six hundred years ago a monastery was founded at the bend of the Ustye River, some twelve miles out of Rostov.

The walls were originally built of wood, but in the 1520s Vasily III ordered the logs replaced with stone. Grigory Borisov of Rostov, an experienced architect, was put in charge of the reconstruction. By that time he had designed the Cathedral of the Trinity at the Danilov Monastery in Pereslavl-Zalessky, the refectory at the Monastery of St Macarius, churches and refectories at the Kirillo-Belozersk Monastery and those of the Spasokamenny Monastery on Lake Kubenskoye as well as other edifices in the Metropolitan See of Rostov. The grimness and austerity of the time in which Borisov lived were reflected in his work. His plain, massive walls were sparsely decorated with bands and narrow pilasters and equipped with loop-holes for firing cannon. He used only brick, no white stone. All embellishments such as ornamental bands, lines of "skittles" and vertically set stone, the niches and triangles were hewn of brick which was made near the building site.

Evidently the walls and towers of Borisoglebsky were built in sections, not all at the same time. About the mid-sixteenth century a large fortress of primary military importance arose on a hill among the pine trees. Its walls were approximately 10 feet thick and 40 feet high. There were fourteen towers, circular ones, with observation platforms at the corners, and rectangular ones between them. They were placed at intervals equal to an arrow's flight. Bows and arrows were still in use in the sixteenth century. The walls and towers had projections for the long cannon of the time, and above them firing platforms and embrasures for the archers.

There are two gateways in the wall. Each had four pairs of heavy oak doors reinforced with iron. All that is left of them are the massive hooks in the walls. In the south gateway there are traces of the slits by means of which the grating was let down. The entrance ways at the north and south gates are now quite straight, but originally they must have been zigzagged in order to impede the enemy's attempts to force their way in. Later we shall see such an entrance at the Pilgrim's Tower at Zagorsk.

On three sides Borisoglebsky was protected by the River Ustye and a deep pond. On the fourth there had evidently been a moat — vestiges of it are still visible. The fortifications in Borisoglebsky are the oldest and strongest of any on the Golden Ring, almost as strong as those of the Moscow Kremlin, although smaller in size, with a perimeter of 3,380 feet. The fortress escaped damage during the peasant uprisings and during the Polish invasion early in the seventeenth century. The Polish and Livonian armies maneuvered around it for two years. They burned out the settlement adjoining the Monastery, but failed to take the fortress.

After getting the work started on the fortifications, Grigory Borisov laid the foundation of the Cathedral of Sts Boris and Gleb, which he completed in 1524. It was the custom for the cathedral to occupy the centre of the monastery grounds, but in Borisoglebsky the edifice was placed to the side, toward the north-east corner of the wall. This was done for defence purposes as at that time the cavalry was of primary importance and a great deal of open space was needed for quartering the men and taking care of the horses.

Narrow pilasters divide the walls of the plain, squat, rectangular body of the single-domed cathedral with three almost semicircular apses. The original covering over the *zakomaras* was replaced in the eighteenth century by a hipped roof. A drum was added at the same time, but the work was crudely done. A pretentious structure resembling a tall hat was substituted for the helmet-shaped dome. A century later a chapel was attached to the west portal. None of this enhanced the austere contours of the old cathedral.

Inside the walls had been covered with frescoes, the latest painted in 1911 by Yegorov, who had been inspired by the work of Russia's famous artist Victor Vasnetsov. Traces of the old frescoes were found in 1956 by the architect Ognev. The building is due for restoration in the near future.

Rostov's celebrated architect and stone mason Grigory Borisov was responsible for many more buildings in Borisoglebsky. His best effort was the Gate-church of St Sergius. The architect's new and distinctive approach to its construction laid the foundation of Rostov architecture in the sixteenth and seventeenth centuries: the tall five-domed square body of the church was flanked on either side by a heavy, hexagonal tower resembling a helmeted warrior.

The four-pillared church with a double row of windows is a plain, dignified building. Narrow pilasters are asymmetrically disposed on the walls in the typical Borisov manner. Each narrow window is framed in a small cylinder topped by a tiny ogee-shaped *kokoshnik*. The drum columns are girdled by blind arcading. The apse is small, its outlines barely indicated.

Inside the monastery grounds there are six more buildings erected by Borisov in the first half of the sixteenth century – the Church of the Annunciation (1526), the Refectory, the Prior's Residence, the Dormitory, the Wafer Bakery and the Treasury.

The Church of the Annunciation, which is the Prior's house chapel, is connected to the Refectory and the Abbot's Chambers. It is set on a high basement and has a low rectangular apse. The Prior's Residence is a rare example of sixteenth-century civic architecture. Unfortunately it has undergone a great deal of reconstruction, which changed its appearance for the worse.

The Wafer Bakery and Treasury are small, simply designed buildings. Legend has it that the Bakery contained a dungeon, an essential part of every monastery and fortress. Part of its basement is covered by four pendentives resting on a massive pillar.

The Dormitory, a stone structure resting on a high basement, has recently been cleared of the earth which had encased it. Judging by the columns or pilasters (difficult to tell which because of so much reconstruction), it appears that the basement used to serve as living quarters of a dwelling which had one more story made of wood, according to building methods practiced in the sixteenth century and earlier.

A two-story stone building (possibly the old Prior's Residence) was undoubtedly a medieval stronghold. The usual rounded embrasures for the guns are still in evidence on the north wall.

In the 1660s the Metropolitan Jonah, having started the construction of his own court and kremlin at Rostov, used some of the architectural features characteristic of Borisoglebsky.

Still in Jonah's time the Borisoglebsky Fortress-Monastery fell into decay, and was renovated by the prelate's craftsmen, who in the course of restoration dismantled and rebuilt the north-western tower in a style utterly unlike the rest of the ensemble. A new Church of the Purification appeared over the Water Gates on the north side, with contours very much like those of the Church of the Resurrection in the Rostov kremlin. And again we see the two flanking towers! Thus the brilliant architectural device conceived by Grigory Borisov found its way back to Borisoglebsky.

The Metropolitan's stone masons also reconstructed the Holy Gates. They linked the towers with a decorative gallery adorned with a band of rectangular niches, and in the five arched openings they placed ten pendants.

All of the four churches in the kremlin built by the Metropolitan Jonah have a stone barrier instead of a wooden iconostasis separating the altar from the main body of the church. That is another feature borrowed from the Church of St Sergius.

The old Church of the Annunciation with the Refectory built in the reign of Boris Godunov was also remodelled in the late sixteen hundreds. A covered porch was added at the western end and embellished with *kokoshnik* gables and niches inlaid with polychrome tiles and bosses.

The last to be built was the three-tiered bell-tower (1680) with the Church of St John the Forerunner on the ground story. Topped with three small domes, it has a certain similarity with the bell-tower in Rostov, but its lines were even more graceful and light. A covered porch was added – much like the one at the Church of the Annunciation, with tiles and hanging bosses.

29. *Borisoglebsky Monastery. The Gate-church of St Sergius. 1545*

30. *Borisoglebsky Monastery. The Church of the Purification-over-the-Water-gate. C.1680*

31. *Borisoglebsky Monastery. The Gate-church of St Sergius. Portal arches of the Holy Gates and galleries. Latter half of the 17th century*

32. *View of the Borisoglebsky Monastery*

33. *Borisoglebsky Monastery. Western wall with towers. Mid-16th century →*

NIKOLA-ULEIMA

There is a tranquil beauty about the Yaroslavl Region. It is perhaps most pleasant there in the vicinity of the Monastery of St Nicholas-on-the-Uleima about nine miles out of Uglich. Travelling from Rostov Veliky we see golden fields of grain, double rows of birches on each side of the road, log-houses scattered on the hillocks, and the crystal-clear, reed-bordered Uleima River. At the water's edge there are little log bath-houses. There are plenty of lime-trees on the knoll across the river. Visible through their foliage are the time-weathered walls of the Monastery of St Nicholas-on-the-Uleima and the domes of its churches.

One of the bloodiest episodes of the Polish invasion of Muscovy took place at the Monastery. Lime-trees are aged and perhaps the oldest of them remember when Hetman Sapieha's men attacked the fortress-monastery.

The Monastery was founded in 1400 as a look-out post on the road to Uglich. A stockade was put up, a moat dug, and low ramparts built. It wasn't much of a stronghold. When Hetman Sapieha swooped down upon it in 1608, he expected it to fall at once. But the few dozen men-at-arms, the monks, and the inhabitants of neighbouring villages who had taken refuge within the monastery walls were determined to resist to the last man. Even Father Superior Varsonofy, an old man, took sabre in hand, recalling the fighting days of his youth.

For several days the little company held off the enemy. When the invaders broke into the flaming monastery premises, the defenders locked themselves in the cathedral. They resisted until the undermined and burning walls and vaulting collapsed and every man, woman and child were buried beneath the ruins. Even the following day, according to eye-witnesses' accounts, agonized moans could still be heard.

The Cathedral of St Nicholas was reconstructed in 1675 on the old foundation and surviving walls. The Church of the Presentation in the Temple, which had sustained less damage than the other buildings during the siege, was completely rebuilt twenty years later.

The low, five-domed Cathedral is typical of Yaroslavl architecture in the latter half of the seventeenth century. Inside frescoes have been discovered beneath paintings of little artistic value. They will soon be cleaned and restored.

The Church of the Presentation in the Temple is of greater interest. Rising on a high basement, it is a graceful structure surmounted by a hipped roof, its outer walls divided by pilasters and richly moulded *kokoshnik* gables. The elegant drum and helmet-shaped dome belong to the eighteenth century. The altar is of a most unusual cylindrical shape. A refectory added on the western side has a bell-tower over it with arched apertures in the bell section, and slit windows on the octagonal tent-shaped roof with vertical projecting ridges. Adjoining the cathedral on the north side is the Dormitory with a double-door porch, flights of steps forming inclined arches, rectangular recesses, and niches on the parapet. In both the Cathedral of St Nicholas and the Church of the Presentation it is difficult to say with any accuracy which architectural features belong to the sixteenth and which to the seventeenth century. The two buildings are now undergoing research and restoration.

The Gate-church of the Trinity, built in the early eighteenth century, has been altered a number of times. The wooden walls of the Monastery, which were erected during the same period, had never been of military importance. The low towers of circular, rectangular and cubic shape are highly ornamental, with pilaster strips, panels and polychrome tiling. The builders of the monastery must have possessed talent and good taste. During the lifetime of Peter the Great they created a shrine that may have been archaic, but it was dear to the people of Yaroslavl, and harmonized beautifully with the softness of the Central Russian landscape – the winding streams, the white birches and dark-green lime-trees.

34. *The Monastery of St Nicholas-on-the-Uleima. 16th–18th centuries* →

UGLICH

At the end of the sixteenth century, in the kremlin at Uglich, the Tsarina's Palace had a solitary occupant – Maria Nagaya, the seventh and last wife of Ivan the Terrible, was living there in honorary exile. It was in her palace garden that Tsarevich Dmitry met his death on May, 15, 1591. The Uglich tragedy is associated in the minds of the Russian readers with Pushkin's *Boris Godunov.*

> I at that time was sent to Uglich
> Upon some mission. I arrived at night,
> Next morning at the hour of holy mass,
> I heard upon a sudden a bell toll;
> 'Twas the alarm bell. Then a cry, an uproar;
> Men rushing to the court of the Tsarina . . .

The tsarevich, a sickly boy, was the last of the Rurik dynasty. The mystery of his death will probably never be solved. Perhaps he stabbed himself in an epileptic fit. Or he might have been killed by assassins sent by Boris Godunov. All we know is that a certain Kleshnin, one of the court attendants, was generously rewarded by Godunov, and rumour had it that Kleshnin was the man who had engineered the assassination.

Soon after the tragic event a little chapel went up on the spot where Dmitry had bled to death. The wooden Church of St Demetrius-on-the-Blood was built there in 1630. It was replaced in 1692 by the present red and white stone building similar in style to the Moscow churches of the mid-seventeenth century, with a cluster of five domes over the square-shaped body of the main part, ornamental *zakomaras,* richly moulded cornices, paired columns at the corners, highly decorative surrounds at all the windows including those of the low refectory and semicircular apses. The octagonal belfry rests on a square base and is topped by a tent-shaped spire. The covered parvis and north chapel added later are not large enough to detract from the pleasing outlines of the building. The church itself and the crypt below it have now been turned into a museum.

The cathedral in the Uglich kremlin was constructed in 1713. In Yaroslavl we shall see a number of churches which served as a model for it. Its finest architectural feature is the five-domed crown.

The bell-tower, added in 1730, is the tallest building in the kremlin. Its somewhat archaic form consists of three gradually diminishing octagons in the "Naryshkin" style of architecture prevalent in and around Moscow during the last two decades of the seventeenth century.

It is interesting that in 1730 another building, the Korsun Church, rose in Uglich with the same Moscow-type bell-tower. Set on a square base, it has tall slender drums supporting a cluster of domes topped by crosses on elongated needle-like spires.

All that remains of the Tsarina's Court is the building known as the Palace of Tsarevich Dmitry. The two-story stone structure with a double-hipped roof was erected in the fifteenth century by Prince Andrei Bolshoi (the Big), who as a result of a feud with his elder brother Grand Prince Ivan III ended his days in prison.

The Palace of Tsarevich Dmitry is the oldest building in Uglich and is of the greatest historical value. It is tall and simply designed with smooth walls devoid of whitewash. The pediments are embellished with ornamental bands of brickwork and terracotta. All this patterned carving on the smooth surface of the walls is reminiscent of folk-style embroidered towels. When the Palace was restored in the last century, the roof was covered with sheets of copper, which darkened with time and now blend in with the rest of the structure. But the porches of pseudo-Russian style do not seem to belong to this stately building.

We find the most interesting architectural treasures of Uglich outside the kremlin.

The Church of the Nativity of St John the Baptist, built in 1689–1700, was immortalized by Nikolai Roerich, a Russian painter; his well-known picture represents the sturdy pillar of the porch and an arch with the laconic inscription: "Uglich".

The layout, construction and decoration of the church are of the usual type. The square-shaped body of the edifice rests on a high basement and is equipped with the customary five domes, several chapels, a tent-shaped bell-tower, a staircase, and a porch with jar-like pillars. Its charm lies in the faultless balance and harmony achieved by the unknown architect between the various elements of the building. The church is magnificent from every angle, seen at a distance or close up, in overcast or sunny weather.

And now we turn to the Monastery of the Resurrection across the road from the Church of St John. It is the work of Russian crafts-men begun in 1674 under instructions from the Metropolitan Jo-nah. The Cathedral of the Resurrection, the Bell-tower, the Refec-tory, together with the Church of Our Lady of Smolensk, all stand in line forming a single ensemble. The cathedral stands on the customary basement. The covered gallery, the high porch with four pillars, the arches with pendants are all features prescribed by the Metropolitan Jonah. The bell-tower is practically a copy of the one at Borisoglebsky. The single-domed Church of Our Lady of Smol-ensk has a stone altar reminding us of churches in the Rostov kremlin. The tower-like little belfry also takes us back to Rostov.

From the Volga River we get a lovely view of Uglich with the Cathedral of the Resurrection and St John's Church looming on the horizon. In the heart of the town among the rather ordinary eccle-siastical buildings there is another church in honour of the Virgin of Smolensk. Although completed in 1700, it is built in the tradi-tions of the sixteen hundreds.

The few surviving examples of old secular architecture include the two-story stone houses of the Kalashnikov family (early eighteenth century), and the Ovsiannikov family of merchants (1760–70). Both reflect building trends of St Petersburg in its early days. Another example is the Voronin house, which formerly belonged to the Mekhov family. It is also a two-story structure, but built of wood. The tile stove which still stands on the ground floor is an unmatched piece of art.

The Monastery of St Alexis, the oldest in Uglich, was founded in 1371 by Alexis, Metropolitan of All Russia, an important political figure in the state of Muscovy. It was sacked and burned down during the Polish and Lithuanian invasion early in the seventeenth century. The monastery was rebuilt in the 1620s. One of the buildings on the premises, the Church of St John the Baptist, is typical of the period and in no way remarkable. But another one dedicated to the Dormition of the Virgin (1628) is a magnificent structure. Small in size, it adjoins the plain, two-story Refectory with a spacious single-pillared chamber on the first floor. The church is of simple design – three square blocks merged into one, and above them three octagons each of which is topped by a faceted tent-like spire. The larger central spire, encircled by a band of *kokoshniks,* towers over the two flanking it. All three are surmounted by slender drums supporting scale-covered cupolas. The three apses below have a cornice of indented cut stone and are embellished with an unusual band of blind arcading. It is all very elegant and perfectly proportioned.

The church known for centuries as "Divnaya" (Wondrous) has always been dear to the hearts of the people of Uglich. Its slender triple-spired silhouette can be seen from every part of town. It is said that people used to stand in front of it and exclaim "Divnaya!" Most residents have probably forgotten that originally this beautiful church of the St Alexis Monastery had been named in honour of the Dormition of the Virgin.

The town itself has always been among the most beloved in old Russia. Legend has it that one of the Uglich bells was whipped and exiled to Siberia for sounding the alarm and rising the inhabitants of Uglich to rebellion on the day of the tsarevich's assassination.

35. *Uglich. The kremlin. The Church of St Demetrius-on-the-Blood. 1690–92*

36. *Uglich. The kremlin. The Church of St Demetrius-on-the-Blood. 1690–92. Fresco*

38. *Uglich. The Monastery of St Alexis. 17th century*

39. *Uglich. The Church of the Nativity of St John the Baptist-on-the-Volga.
1689–1700* →

TUTAYEV

The history of the little town of Tutayev on the Volga, formerly known as Romanov-Borisoglebsk, goes back over 700 years. It begins in the middle of the thirteenth century when Prince Roman, the great-grandson of Grand Prince Vsevolod-the-Big-Nest, was granted this rural area. The area was centred around the village of Borisoglebsk on the right bank of the Volga.

Across the river from it the young prince built a fortified town on the high ravine-furrowed bank. We can still see the moat and ramparts that surrounded it. Homes for the prince's personal troop of warriors were put up in the vicinity. That is how the custom started for noblemen and men-at-arms to settle at Romanov and for common folk such as fishermen, farmers, and furriers (famous for dressing the fine local sheepskin) to settle at Borisoglebsk. Later the two settlements merged into the district town of Romanov-Borisoglebsk. In 1921 the name was changed to Tutayev in honour of the Red Army hero.

It seems that every old town has something inexplicable about it. In Tutayev we wonder why the large and splendid Cathedral of the Resurrection stands amidst the humble cottages on the Borisoglebsk side. It would be understandable if it were erected at Romanov which for centuries had belonged to the princes and noblemen. But it is on record that the cathedral had been built by "Mikita Malodushkin . . . Zakhar Kuzmin . . . Kornil and Matfey Fiodorov, and all the peasants of the Borisoglebsk settlement."

The Cathedral was erected in the 1670s on the foundation of an older twelfth-century church. Arcaded galleries surround the building on three sides. The porches and staircases were moved to the side. However, the asymmetrical position of the porches only enhanced the strict symmetry of the central structure.

The galleries, the walls of the rectangular body of the church, the apses, and drums with the round domes characteristic of Yaroslavl architecture are completely covered with ornamental brickwork and tiling. As we shall see later only the churches of Kostroma and Yaroslavl are decorated on such a lavish scale.

The low, tent-shaped bell-tower is a graceful structure, and imitations of its tiered gate-tower soon appeared in Yaroslavl, in the architectural complexes of Tolchkovo and Korovnikova Sloboda.

The frescoes covering the interior walls are well preserved. One can gaze upon them for hours on end admiring the unknown Yaroslavl artists for their skill in investing biblical scenes with living characters and for their distinctive interpretation of beauty. In *The Tower of Babel* we not only get an idea of the confusion caused by the sudden lack of understanding among the workers, but also of seventeenth-century technology. *The Last Judgement* and *Tortures of Hell* are balanced by scenes of absolution for sinners, indicating that humanism has always been a part of the Russian character.

There are six churches on the left bank of the river. The oldest is the Cathedral of the Exaltation of the Cross, which stands "on the ramparts" on the site of an old fortified settlement. Further up the river is the Spaso-Arkhangelskaya Church and beyond it the Church of the Transfiguration and the Virgin of Kazan. The Church of the Intercession is the last one on the left. All of them belong to the seventeenth and early eighteenth centuries. Modest and unassuming they make no pretence of competing with the magnificent Cathedral of the Resurrection. Each has its own tent-shaped bell-tower either attached or standing by itself. The most interesting is the Church of the Transfiguration and the Virgin of Kazan clinging to a steep hillside.

The six buildings have the appearance of royal watch-towers along the Volga. The ravines in between them are overgrown with grass, shrubbery, thickly-crowned maples, and birches with trunks that seem whiter than anywhere else in northern Russia. Down the side of the ravine water trickles from a clear, cold spring, beneath which someone has put a bottomless wooden tub to catch the flow. There are a number of squat houses in the vicinity, some of them bearing the imprint of a talented builder.

40. *Tutayev. The Cathedral of the Resurrection. C. 1670*

41. *Tutayev. The Cathedral of the Resurrection. C. 1670. Fresco: The Tower of Babel. Late 17th century*

YAROSLAVL

The city of Yaroslavl on the Volga is nearly one thousand years old. In the year of 1010 Prince Yaroslav the Wise founded a fortified town on the spot known as the "Bear's Corner" where the Kotorosl River enters the Volga. Legend has it that Prince Yaroslav once killed a bear here with a pole-axe.

The bear, which the original settlers regarded as a sacred animal, appears on the emblem of Yaroslavl Province. Today the picture of a bear greets us on the highway as we enter the town.

In the seventeenth century Yaroslavl reached the peak of its development. It was then that the architectural ensembles went up which made Yaroslavl one of the most beautiful cities of old Russia, with churches rich in frescoes and ceramic ornamentation.

As soon as we come in to town on the road from Moscow, we get a lovely view of the walls and towers of the Monastery of the Transfiguration of Our Saviour and the golden domes of its sixteenth-century cathedral. Particularly impressive is the seventeenth-century Church of the Epiphany decorated with coloured tiles which shine brightly like jewels.

Aside from the cathedral, all that remains of the sixteenth century are the reconstructed bell-tower, the Holy Gates with the clock-tower, and the Refectory, the largest and most convenient quarters for formal receptions. The walls and towers were added in the following century and somewhat later came the Prior's Residence and the Dormitory.

We can see a number of remarkable buildings near the monastery. The monumental Church of the Archangel Michael stands on the Kotorosl Embankment on the site of a former palace. It marked the boundary line between the kremlin and the market-place which began "at the moat beyond the ramparts". The Church of Our Saviour-on-the-Town built by the townspeople is situated on the market square itself and is famous for the great variety of historical scenes depicted in the frescoes inside the church.

Higher up the river bank is the Church of St Nicholas-on-the-Logs (the name derives from the original wooden town), a simple building almost devoid of decoration, yet well-proportioned, with the pointed spire of its bell-tower creating an impression of buoyancy. This type of church was very popular in the Yaroslavl region; we shall find many village shrines patterned on it.

In the distance we see another Church of St Nicholas. There are ten churches in Yaroslavl dedicated to St Nicholas, the patron saint of commerce. It is not surprising since most of the town's population depended on trade and the river for a living. The church, an earlier structure than those mentioned above, was the gift of Nadei Sveteshnikov, a wealthy merchant whose agents travelled to Pskov, Yakutsk and Mangazeya. The plan and composition of the Church of St Nicholas served as a pattern for later structures. Inside there are some very fine frescoes painted in the 1650s by Liubim Ageyev and his team from the town of Kostroma.

The adjacent Church of the Nativity has the same square body as St Nicholas's Church (with the vaulting supported by four pillars), the two chapels and gallery. It was erected on funds donated by the Guryev family of merchants (a town on the Caspian Sea was named after them). The Guryevs carried on trade in Bokhara, and people with imagination used to say that they transformed the gold of the Samarkand sun, the emerald green of the country, and the turquoise blue of the minarets into the walls of the Church of the Nativity on the northern banks of the Volga River. The polychrome tiling soon became a distinctive feature of Yaroslavl churches.

The most important church in honour of the Prophet Elijah is situated in the town's central square like the hub of a wheel with streets branching out of it. The outside walls ornamented with tiling are very beautiful, and the frescoes on the walls and vaulting inside constitute a veritable museum of old Russian painting. The work was done 300 years ago by the well-known artists from Kostroma, Gury Nikitin and Sila Savin. Fifty years later the local craftsman Semionov decorated the cathedral parvis with frescoes.

Let us look at some of the other churches. In the north side of town among rickety fences and tall weeds there are the Church of

St Nicholas-the-Wet and its "twin", the winter Church of Our Lady of Tikhvin. The rich brightly coloured ceramic work that adorns the cornices, surrounds, wall surfaces and the faceted tent-shaped roofs of the chapels is a marvellous sight even for Yaroslavl. The local decorators seem to have been inspired by the fabulous beauty and gem-like glow of oriental rugs. Yet the town has more treasures which can compete with these.

In sharp silhouette against the sky in the morning or evening is a group of ancient buildings on a high bank of the Volga. The two churches, the wall with entrance gate, and the bell-tower make up the famous Korovnikova Sloboda ensemble built in 1654 and decorated at the end of the century with all the colourful magnificence characteristic of the Church of St Nicholas-the-Wet.

Across the Kotorosl River there is another group of churches with the renowned Tolchkovo Church. Seen from a distance it appears to have three domes, but a closer look reveals fifteen, set in clusters on tall, slender drums. The building glows with a rare blend of frescoes, ornamental brick, terracotta and glazed tiles. Everything is decorated – the windows, shutters, doors and porch pediments!

On Tugova Hill to the left of the village of Tolchkovo rises the little single-domed Church of St Paraskeva. It stands above the mass grave of Yaroslavl warriors who fell in battle against the Tartars. To the right of it we can admire the superb silhouette of the white, five-domed Church of St Theodore. Further on there is the Church of St Nicholas Pensky, and beyond it we can just make out the outlines of the St Nicholas-at-Melenki Church. The walls of practically every one of these buildings are covered with frescoes.

There is a large number of frescoes in the Church of the Presentation of the Virgin in the fourteenth-century Tolgsky Monastery. The church is a seventeenth-century structure as are the enormous bell-tower, refectory, and infirmary. None of the earlier monastery buildings have survived.

Monasteries in medieval Russia were more than fortresses and treasury-houses. They served as infirmaries, poor-houses, and foundling homes. The schools there were the only ones in the country. The monks recorded the events of the day making it possible to trace the history of Russia in the chronicles preserved in the monastery archives.

Late in the eighteenth century Count Musin-Pushkin, a distinguished archaeologist, was looking through a bundle of dusty, mildewed books and parchments brought to his attention. While deciphering a sixteenth-century manuscript, he realized that it was a copy of an earlier tale which the transcriber had not fully understood and had interpreted in his own way.

"Yet Boyan, my brothers, did not let loose ten falcons on a flock of swans, but laid his own wizard fingers on the living strings, which then themselves throbbed out praise for the princes. . ."The manuscript proved to be the famous *Lay of Igor's Host*.

The town, which has given us this gem of old Russian literature, is growing bigger and more prosperous. But the centre of old Yaroslavl is being preserved in its original state with the new districts planned so as not to obstruct the town's history and culture.

42. *Yaroslavl. The Monastery of the Transfiguration of Our Saviour with the Church of the Epiphany in the foreground* →

43. *Yaroslavl. The Church of St Paraskeva on Tugova Hill. 1692* ⇒

44. *Yaroslavl. The Monastery of the Transfiguration of Our Saviour. The Dormitory*

45. *Yaroslavl. The Church of St Nicholas-the-Wet. Tent-shaped roof of a chapel. C. 1690*

51. *Yaroslavl. The Church of St John the Baptist at Tolchkovo. 1671–87. Tile decoration*

52. *Yaroslavl. The Church of St John the Baptist at Tolchkovo. 1671–87. Holy Gates*

KOSTROMA

Blue skies over silver waters, a small boat with sails fluttering in the wind . . . This picture decorates the emblem of Kostroma. In the olden times Kostroma was known as "the flax capital of the north"; it supplied Western Europe with the world's finest sail-cloth.

A good deal of trade went on between Kostroma and the West. Once, so the story goes, a small barrel of gold pieces was found in a shipment of dyes sent from England to the firm of the merchant Isakov in exchange for linen goods. A letter was duly dispatched apprising the London company of the discovery. The answer was: "Use the gold for charitable deeds." And so in 1652 Kiril Isakov built the lovely Church of the Resurrection-on-the-Debre on the outskirts of town near one of his own jetties. This story probably explains why bas-reliefs of the heraldic British lion and unicorn appear on the triple-tented portal gate of the church wall along with representations of fabulous birds from Russian folklore. The Church of the Resurrection-on-the-Debre is not only the most beautiful of the old buildings in Kostroma, but one of the finest surviving specimens of seventeenth-century Russian architecture. Although the design of the building is not unusual, the compositional conception of the layout and structure is magnificent. Its main body rests on a four-pillared square base and has five domes over a gently sloping hipped roof. A covered gallery runs along three sides. At the north-western end there is the Chapel of Three Bishops with a triple-pitched roof surmounted by a small cupola. Three ornate tent-shaped porches with hanging bosses in the arches lead to the gallery.

The exterior is lavishly adorned. There are paired demi-columns along the walls, elaborate surrounds over the large windows crowned with tiny *kokoshniks,* and a wide, carved cornice topped by ornamental arches. The walls used to be covered with paintings in alternate squares.

The interior compares favourably with that of any church in the Moscow Kremlin. Frescoes, most of which have been cleaned and restored, decorate the walls and vaulted ceiling. There are a number of icons dating from the fifteenth to the seventeenth centuries. The carved white-stoned recessed portals of the main entrance are pleasing to the eye.

The exquisitely carved iconostasis of the Chapel of Three Bishops is a real gem. One detail is extremely rare in old Russian architecture – the corbels in the shape of hands supporting the tiers of the iconostasis.

The oldest building in the town is the cathedral of the former Monastery of Epiphany (1565). We note here the influence of the Moscow school.

The only residential building remaining from the seventeenth century is the one where the monks used to live. It has been but slightly distorted by additions made over the centuries. All that is left of the wall is one tower, which has been turned into a belfry.

There are three more seventeenth-century churches of interest in Kostroma. Two of them, situated across the Volga, are the Church of the Transfiguration (1685) and the Church of St Elijah-at-the-Gorodishche (1683–85). The former is decorated after the Church of the Resurrection-on-the-Debre with the inside walls covered with frescoes and the exterior adorned with a variety of sculptural details. In contrast, the Church of the Prophet Elijah is sparsely decorated, but beautifully proportioned and well placed on the highest point of the right bank of the Volga.

The Church of St John the Divine standing near the Ipatyevsky Monastery was built in 1687. The construction is typical of the period – a high, square-shaped body with a low refectory, which also functioned as the winter church. The attached bell-tower has the appearance of a gateway tower. Its first tier serves as a parvis with portals on three sides. The octagon above with arched apertures is the bell-tier, and over it there is the tent-shaped roof with projecting ridges along the ribs. The four rows of rectangular and round "windows" of the roof is something we seldom see.

Another distinctive feature is the railing with the bars thrust upward like tongues of flame. The railing was built in 1765–66 by the blacksmiths of Kostroma.

The large number of ancient icons in the iconostasis are worthy of close study, as are the frescoes, one of the last commissions executed by the local team of "Fiodor Loginov and sons with assistants". The date of execution and the names of the artists are inscribed on the north wall.

The pride of Kostroma is the Museum at the former Ipatyevsky Monastery, which played a part in almost every important event of the town's history. The Chronicles of the Ipatyevsky Monastery, a most valuable historical and literary relic, were found in the monastery's archives.

The monastery itself was founded in the fourteenth century by the Zernov family of feudal lords, who were the forebearers of the Godunovs. The crypt of the monastery cathedral became the Godunov burial vault. At one time it held over fifty stone coffins.

The stone wall with a number of towers and the fortress, a formidable one for the sixteenth century, were erected during the reign of Ivan the Terrible.

The Trinity Cathedral was built by relatives of Boris Godunov. They contributed generously toward its appointments including about one hundred icons, most of them with gold mountings. After Boris became tsar, he spared no effort to make the monastery one of the richest in the country.

In the turbulent years of the early seventeenth century the walls of the Ipatyevsky Monastery were blackened by the smoke of gunfire; the ground soaked in blood. Twice the monastery was seized by Polish invaders and Polish battle-standards waved on the wall towers. The fortress witnessed the betrayal of Galich and Kostroma boyars, and also the staunch loyalty of the townspeople.

For six months, the monastery, taken over by the bands of the Second False Dmitry, was besieged. But it withstood the assault and in the end routed the invaders.

Mikhail Romanov, the first of the Romanov Dynasty, left the Ipatyevsky Monastery for Moscow early in the sixteen hundreds to become Tsar of Russia. The pale, timid youth had been elected "not because he was the best choice, but because he was the most expedient". The Romanov boyars, like the Godunovs, were big land-owners in Kostroma.

It was in the winter of 1649, a time of peace, that the towns-people were awakened by a frightful roar caused by an explosion of gun-powder which was kept in the crypt of the Trinity Cathedral. The damaged building, however, was speedily restored and today appears in its original state. We can even admire the old bronze doors incised with gold, which escaped injury during the explosion. The carved, five-tiered iconostasis is of considerable artistic merit, but the cathedral's most striking feature are the frescoes which cover the walls, pillars and vaulting like a bright fabric. "This church," reads an item in the church records, "was decorated with paintings in the summer of 7194 (1686)." The well-known Gury Nikitin and his assistants were in charge of the work.

Among the old buildings of interest on the monastery grounds are the Bishop's Palace (1588), the Prior's Residence (also sixteenth century), and the Refectory (1640).

The enormous five-tiered bell-tower is an outstanding speci-men of sixteenth-century architecture as well as the cathedral. Orig-inally the tower was built by Dmitry Godunov, a kinsman of the Tsar, but a number of additions were made later. Its highest plat-form offers a glorious view of the town and its vicinity, and of the first outdoor museum of wooden architecture in the Soviet Union.

The museum contains the rectangular, cottage-like church from the village of Spas-Vezhi; it stands on high wooden piles to protect it from spring floods. The bath-house nearby is also set up on piles. There are also another wooden church; the wind-mill, a two-story structure, possibly the last of its kind in Russia; the four-hundred-year-old Church of the Virgin (1552) from the village of Kholm; and an ordinary peasant dwelling from Kologriv.

From the bell-tower we can also see the monument dedicated to their famous countryman Ivan Susanin. The memorial overlook-ing the Volga is a symbol of courage, fortitude and patriotism.

Today Kostroma is known as the only city in the Soviet Union which has retained the layout formed in its central part during the eighteenth and early nineteenth century.

In the 1770s, Russian towns were being re-planned on a large scale. Some 400 general plans were submitted. The one for Kostroma was sanctioned in 1784 and put into effect in practically every detail. The great fire of 1773, which destroyed all the wooden buildings, served to facilitate the project. The work of reconstruction was done on land that was razed to the ground.

The Roman architect Vitruvius Pollio, who lived in the first century B.C., in his work *De architectura,* said that a town situated on a seashore or riverbank should start from that point. The architects of Kostroma followed that advice. The open end of the central U-shaped square faces the Volga and the streets fan out from there. Buildings at that time were placed according to a sanctioned plan. Corner areas were the first to be built up to serve as guide lines for the new streets. With so many irregularly shaped plots of land involved, most of the "approved", but actually standard projects, had to be readjusted to fit into the radial plan. This was to the town's advantage, since individual treatment gave the buildings character and distinction. Some of them have been carefully preserved to this day as valuable architectural monuments.

The square on the bank of the Volga was set aside for trade. The construction of the Krasnye and Bolshiye Muchnye Stalls started in 1789 according to the plan and under the supervision of the local architect S. Vorotilov. The Krasnye Stalls, forming a rectangle (about 400 by 530 ft.), dealt in fabrics, footwear, and various fancy goods. Along the perimeter of the mart there is a covered gallery with tall arches supported by strong pillars, and in the centre of the main façade a triangular portico with similar arches. There used to be a gallery on the courtyard side as well, but a few arches are all that remained of it. The Bolshiye Stalls offered flour, grain, fodder, and Kostroma's traditional product, flax. Extending over an area of some 365 by 520 feet, they resemble the

Krasnye Stalls except for the lower part of the pillars which is broader. Later on ten more trading booths were added for the sale of cakes, corn, fish, oil, tobacco and other products. Some of them were placed next to each other on the same area, while others occupied space in the courtyards of older structures.

The fine buildings erected early in the past century along the outside of the square enhanced its appearance and gave it the look of a finished ensemble. First let us take note of the splendid eight-columned Borshchov Mansion, which used to be the property of General Borshchov who fought in the War of 1812.

A veritable palace, it is the largest of all the residential buildings constructed in Kostroma by private citizens. A bit to the side there is a fire-tower which is still used as such. The tower is a magnificent piece of architecture; particularly impressive is the central cube with a portico of the Corinthian order on a high base, with an octagonal white-stone patrol tower. The graceful and highly imaginative structure over a hundred feet high is most imposing against the low arcade of trading stalls.

Between the Borshchov Mansion and the fire-tower we see what is now a library. In its place stood the wooden building of a guard-house erected in 1797. Later it was replaced with a new one by the architect Fursov, the designer of the fire-tower. Despite its small size, it charms the viewer with its stately contours, splendid proportions, and skilfully executed architectural details. It graces the square and the town as a whole, and is one of the finest specimens of Russian classic architecture.

59. *Kostroma. Ipatyevsky Monastery. Mansion of the Romanov boyars. 16th–19th centuries*

61, 62. *Kostroma. Ipatyevsky Monastery. The Trinity Cathedral. Designs on the south gates. 16th century*

KRASNOYE-ON-THE-VOLGA

Kostroma and the villages in the vicinity were well known throughout Muscovy for the gold and silver ornaments produced by local jewellers. Their workshops were centred for the most part at the village of Krasnoye on the Volga. Krasnoye was the property of the Viazemsky princes, and before their time it had belonged to the Godunov family of feudal lords.

The Godunovs could not boast of noble lineage. In all probability they came from peasant stock. They were wealthy and reputed to be good managers and enterprising people. In their numerous estates they established jewellery and other workshops, and it may be that the traditions of the jeweller's art, handed down from father to son, have come to us from the Godunov period.

The village of Krasnoye must have had quite a large population. Otherwise the thrifty citizens would not have built such a big and imposing church.

Tent-shaped churches made their appearance in Russia early in the sixteenth century. Every one of the few that have survived is a precious memorial of the past. Perhaps the finest, if not the earliest, is at the village of Kolomenskoye, now within the city limits of Moscow. According to old records the Church of the Epiphany at Krasnoye was patterned after it.

In certain details the church at Krasnoye resembles the central part of the Cathedral of St Basil in Moscow, while the general plan reminds one of the Cathedral of the Transfiguration at Bolshiye Viazemy on the outskirts of Moscow. There is the same arched crypt under the entire building, the same kind of gallery, the same rectangular body with two small chapels surmounted by a pile of *kokoshniks.* The tented roof over the octagon resting on the rectangle is similar to the roof of the Church of the Nativity in the village of Beseda on the Moskva River. Since Krasnoye-on-the-Volga as well as Bolshiye Viazemy and Beseda belonged to the Godunovs, there is a possibility that the churches in all three villages were designed by the same architect. Be that as it may, there is no doubt that the Church of the Epiphany was built by a gifted "supervisor of

144

stone masonry" – an official designation of architects in the sixteenth century.

The creator of the church at Krasnoye set a tapering octagon
over the broad, low rectangular body embellishing the upper structure with two rows of decorative shallow *zakomaras*. He put up a
third tier with a strip of small *kokoshniks*, and at the base of the
tented roof he placed triangular frames enclosing six little *kokoshniks* in each. He topped the tall edifice with a slender drum pierced
with lancet windows and surmounted by a helmet-shaped dome.

The chapel roofing indicates the hand of another architect, or
that the chapels had been altered during the seventeenth-century reconstruction when a second row of arcading was added and the formerly open gallery covered. A bell-tower was added at the same
time and although the builders did their best to make it harmonize
with the church, their efforts were not entirely successful. But if the
tower failed to enhance the general effect, it did not spoil it.

It has always been recognized that the tent-shaped church is the
stone version of the wooden church of Russia's north. Yet in its
sharp outlines there is something in common with the Lutheran
church of Western Europe. That seems to be one of the reasons why
in the seventeenth century Patriarch Nikon banned the tent-shaped
roof. Instead he prescribed the canonical five domes giving the theo-
logical explanation that the lower domes symbolized the four evan-
gelists and the tall one in the middle "the seat of the Lord Himself."

68. *Krasnoye-on-the-Volga. The Church of the Epiphany. 1592* →

69. *Krasnoye-on-the-Volga. The Church of the Epiphany. 1592.
The Archangel Michael from the Deesis (Art Museum, Kostroma). Late 16th century* →

PLIOS

The banks of the Volga are exceptionally lovely at Plios, the little town whose history goes back to the dim and distant past. Plios stands on the site of the ancient fortified settlement of Chuvil.

Vasily I, the son of Dmitry Donskoi, founded the town of Plios in 1410. He ordered the ravines round the old fort deepened and the river bank made steeper. His men put up earthen ramparts as well, and an oak-wood stockade with defensive towers. Vigilance was essential with the hostile Kingdom of Kazan so near, and the towers offered an unobstructed view of the surrounding countryside due to the *plios*, that is the straight part of the river between bends.

The fortress was the first line of defence against enemy attack. The twang of Tartar arrows had resounded within its walls, which had been razed by fire a number of times. The small troop of defenders bolstered by the townspeople fought until the last man perished in a battle against superior forces. But each time the enemy withdrew, the carpenters would take up their axes to repair the damage. Again and again the town rose up from ruins.

Rafts carrying Russian warriors floated past Plios on their way to Kazan and Astrakhan. In the sixteenth century these men cleared the entire area along the Volga of the Mongol hordes.

The mounted troops of the Polish nobleman Lisowski made lightning raids on the town. When the regiments of Minin and Pozharsky came from Nizhni-Novgorod at the time of the spring floods, the people of Plios built rafts to take the men across the river. From there the warriors drove on to Moscow toward victory!

After the borders of Muscovy had spread far to the east and west 300 years ago, there was no longer any need for a stronghold and Plios developed into a quiet little provincial town.

One of the old buildings still standing is the stately, eighteenth-century Church of the Resurrection effectively set on a steep bluff. The rectangular body with faceted apses and a double row of windows is surmounted by five domes. When a refectory, bell-tower, and porticos were added a century later, it was done without distorting the general graceful outlines of the church.

Unfortunately, the reconstruction of another eighteenth-century church done at the same time was by no means successful.

Standing next to it is yet another church built in the classic manner. It is in a dilapidated condition. A Russian version of the Empire style, it is an ordinary wooden structure with stuccowork imitating stone and we can't expect it to last as long as stone. But its proportions, still discernible in the surviving parts, indicate the hand of a gifted architect. What he has created is beautiful even in a half ruined state.

It is difficult to describe the enchanting countryside around Plios. On the walk along the rivershore the scene changes with every turn of the path bringing into view delightful landscapes against the broad sweep of the Volga. The Russian landscape painter Levitan produced one of his finest works here – *Golden Plios in the Evening.* In speaking about it to the painter, Anton Chekhov is quoted as saying "I see that a smile has appeared in your pictures!"

70. *The town of Plios →*

SUZDAL

The snow-white, gold-crowned gerfalcon, symbol of princely rule, is the emblem of Suzdal, capital city of Yury Dolgoruky, the first appanaged prince of the Rostov-Suzdal Principality.

The tour of the town, the guide-book tells us, should begin with the oldest buildings. But such advice is difficult to follow. As soon as we get a glimpse of the light airy steeple of the Church of St Cosmas and St Damian situated on the site of an old pagan temple across the Kamenka River, we forget all about time and schedule. The lovely little church is like a poem in stone!

And when you get to the river, it is well to stand for a bit on the steep bank of the Kamenka and let your soul absorb the beauty around you. You will never forget the red-orange walls of the Spaso-Yevfimiev Monastery, the white, billowing outlines of the Convent of the Intercession, the richly ornamented gates of the Convent of the Deposition of the Robe, the exquisite architecture of the churches, and the bell-towers with the concave silhouette characteristic of the town of Suzdal.

After Kiev fell to the Lithuanians, Suzdal became the religious centre of medieval Rus. Many of the oldest monasteries were there; it was associated with princes Boris and Gleb, Alexander Nevsky, Dmitry Pozharsky, and tsars' wives, who, when no longer in favour, were banished to the convents of Suzdal.

Grand princes and tsars donated large sums for the building and decoration of convents and monasteries. In the *posad* the people themselves erected churches. It is amazing how many they built in such a small town! The churches often stood in pairs – a cold, high-vaulted summer church usually elaborately decorated and next to it a smaller, simpler one for the winter. Neither was heated, but the winter building, possibly with a heating unit of sorts in the altar, the low-vaulted roof, the burning candles and sanctuary lamps created the illusion of warmth.

Immediately upon entering the town we see on the right side of the road the Church of Our Lady of the Sign with a triple ribbon frieze decorating the walls. Adjacent is the bell-tower and the winter

Church of the Deposition of the Robe. Further along, the Church of St Lazarus, oldest of the *posad* churches, built in 1667 by the townspeople. At the market-place in the centre of town rises the main Church of the Resurrection with its imposing octagonal bell-tower decorated with deep rectangular niches lined with poly-chrome glazed tiles. In back of it stands the modest winter Church of Our Lady of Kazan, and to the left the Church of the Entry into Jerusalem, which, bereft of its original five domes, looks much like the Church of St Paraskeva Piatnitsa next to it. To the right there is the Church of the Emperor Constantine. The smooth surface of its walls is embellished with carving – rows of skittle-like orna-mentation, baluster-shaped tiling, horse-shoe-shaped *kokoshniks*, and elaborate window surrounds. The intricate drums of the five domes give full expression to the designer's flair for carved orna-mentation. Paired with the Church of the Emperor Constantine is the extremely plain Church of the Dolorous Virgin. But its simpli-city is relieved by the highly decorative bell-tower, colourful with majolica ornament which looks like strings of red and green beads.

Some of the churches have lost their "twin". The elegant Church of Our Lady of Smolensk, for example, stands alone at the northern gate of the town, next to the seventeenth-century house of Nikita Pustosviat. Other churches, such as the one in the centre of town dedicated to St John the Forerunner, never had an adjacent winter building. Its simple lines are reminiscent of the Pskov and Novgorod schools. The structure is octagonal, set up on a square base and the hipped roof is supported by two sturdy pillars.

Both the Church of the Dormition in the kremlin and the Church of St Boris and St Gleb by the river outside of town are un-doubtedly of the Moscow school of architecture, typical of the "Na-ryshkin" baroque with details resembling the technique of Yakov Bukhvostov, reputed to be Moscow's finest architect in the late sev-enteenth century.

The now shallow Kamenka used to be an important trade route and, according to custom, a wooden church in honour of St

Nicholas once stood at the main jetty in the south-east corner of the kremlin. When the building burned down, it was replaced in 1720 by another one dedicated to the saint. It is a most attractive example of typically Suzdalian architecture. Although only one dome remains of the original five, the church still retains its inexpressible charm. It is so beautiful that we can hardly spare a glance for the small heated Church of the Nativity of Christ just back of it, even though the lines of the "twin" church are pleasing enough.

There are five monasteries in Suzdal. Two of them – the St Alexander and St Basil – have been poorly maintained. The former, it is said, was founded by Alexander Nevsky in the thirteenth century and used to be called the Great Lavra. But the majestic Cathedral of the Ascension built with funds donated by Natalia Naryshkina, mother of Peter the Great, still stands, as does the tall bell-tower similar to that of the Church of the Resurrection.

Not much remains of the St Basil Monastery situated on the outskirts of town on the road to Kideksha – only part of the wall (late seventeenth century), a small cathedral, and the refectory of the Church of the Purification built at the same time.

The entrance to the Convent of the Deposition of the Robe lies through the famous Holy Gates surmounted by two tent-shaped roofs designed by Ivan Mamin, Andrei Shmakov, and Ivan Griaznov who always worked together. These gifted architects knew how to blend rich and varied ornamentation with a clear-cut expressive silhouette. Just behind the gates there is an early sixteenth-century cathedral with walls divided by flat pilaster strips. It has plain narrow windows, ogee-shaped *zakomaras,* and underneath a frieze of pentagonal niches. Pointed double niches encircle the dome drums. The cathedral is crowned with just three domes, since the "sacred five domes" prescribed by the church authorities came into use much later. It seems that other factors besides changing styles determined the number of domes to be erected. Today we know little about the ecclesiastical subtleties which our ancestors understood very well four hundred and fifty years ago. We also don't know the extent of Suzdal's connections with other countries at the time. There is the possibility that the pointed niches and minaret-like drums came to Russia from the east.

The Spaso-Yevfimiev Monastery, Suzdal's largest, is situated on the eastern outskirts of town. It is 600 years old, but its massive, twenty-towered stone wall with a perimeter of about three quarters of a mile is only half that age. The gate of the entrance-tower is not high; the passageway is rather gloomy. You come out in a small courtyard and enter an even lower passage of the Gate-church of the Annunciation dating from the early seventeenth century. And finally there is the large, squat cathedral decorated with frescoes inside and out and topped with big onion domes. Adjoining it is a chapel much like the one next to the Cathedral of St Basil the Blessed in Moscow. It stands over the grave of the Abbot Euthymus (Yevfimy) after whom the monastery was named. Next to the cathedral there is a large belfry with a church "beneath the bells" dedicated to St John the Forerunner. The date of the construction suggests that it may have been built in honour of the birth of Vasily III's first and only son, the future Tsar Ivan the Terrible.

The Church of the Dormition was erected about five years before the famous Church of the Ascension in the village of Kolomenskoye, now within the city limits of Moscow. It is considered the first tent-shaped church in Russia built of stone.

There are many dark pages in the history of the cathedral. Since the time of Catherine the Great it was used as a state prison. Pugachov's followers languished behind its walls, the Decembrist Shakhovskoi died there. Up until the October Revolution the Suzdal Ecclesiastical Prison, as it was called, was not subordinate to the Ministry of Justice. Its very name inspired terror.

After the depressing atmosphere of the monastery it is a relief to come out on the riverbank and to gaze at the lovely panorama of the Convent of the Intercession.

Most of the convent buildings were built early in the sixteenth century with funds contributed by the father of Ivan the Terrible, *159*

Vasily III. He was determined to divorce his wife Solomonia Saburova on the grounds that she was unable to bear children. Divorce proceedings dragged on for fifteen years. Finally, in 1525 she was forced to take the veil and was banished to the Convent of the Intercession.

There is a mausoleum-like austerity about the beautiful tripledome Cathedral of the Intercession, and in the interior the impression is strengthened by the plain whitewashed walls and the floor paved with black ceramic tiles. There are small niches in the lower part of the walls for breviaries and prayer rugs which were lined with cotton wool and had a loop for the left hand. The nuns used the rugs when they prostrated themselves bewailing their unhappy lot and the cruelty of mankind.

The burial vault in the crypt contains the tomb of Solomonia (Sister Sophia), the Tsarina who had fallen from grace. A child's coffin with a rag-doll in it was recently found next to it. According to legend, Solomonia had borne a son at the convent and fearful for his life had entrusted him to faithful friends. She then claimed that the child had died and even staged a mock burial.

Yevdokia Lopukhina, Peter the Great's first wife, was also imprisoned at the Convent of the Intercession.

Two other buildings are of special interest. One is the tiny, toy-like Church of the Annunciation over the main Holy Gate entrance. The other is the refectory-type Church of the Conception.

From the Convent of the Intercession it is pleasant to follow the meadow-path along the north bank of the Kamenka. You will pass the Church of Our Lady of Tikhvin and the Church of the Prophet Elijah standing on higher ground, and view with delight the exquisite little bell-tower of the heated Church of the Nativity and the stately elegance of the adjoining Church of the Epiphany.

An open air museum of old Russian architecture, similar to the one in Kostroma, has been started on the other side of the Kamenka River. It is to be a collection of churches and dwellings built long ago with ax and chisel and covered with aspen-shingled roofs. Some are already in place. The Church of the Transfiguration and the Church of St Nicholas come from the heart of the Suzdal region. An ordinary peasant log-house stands next to them. Another St Nicholas's Church brought from the village of Glotovo has been set back of the tall ramparts of the kremlin, which in itself is an outdoor museum and has been for a long time.

Within its walls is the Cathedral of the Nativity of the Virgin built in the eleventh century by Vladimir Monomachus. It was in a dilapidated state when his great-great-grandson Georgy ordered it dismantled. In 1255, Georgy erected a new sandstone cathedral in its place. Two hundred and twenty years later the top of the cathedral collapsed. It was rebuilt in 1530 and today, after recent restoration and the removal of adjoining structures which had distorted the design, appears much as it did then. It now stands as a memorial of two centuries, the thirteenth and sixteenth. What remains of the earlier period is the lower part of the walls made of rough porous tufa and carved details of the more solid limestone – a band of small columns and deeply-recessed arches as well as the unusual, obviously oriental-type female masks which we shall see later at the town of Bogoliubovo.

Inside the cathedral, fragments of the thirteenth-century frescoes have survived in the upper part of the southern apse and also in the *arcosolia*. Recently traces of the old frescoes have also been on the pillars in front of the altar.

An iconostasis was added late in the seventeenth century – a simple but impressive structure decorated with sheets of gilded silver. The painting was done by court artist Grigory Zinovyev.

The most striking feature of the cathedral are the Golden Gates of the south and west portals. The enormous doors with designs of gold on the dull black background of the bronze panels are a priceless specimen of medieval Russian art. Pictured on the tablets are fabulous beasts, scenes from the Gospels, and even homely scenes such as the one showing an angel instructing a man in the use of a wooden spade.

Our picture of Suzdal will be incomplete unless we see something of its domestic architecture. There is a seventeenth-century stone house which has survived virtually in its original state on Lenin Street. It is said to have belonged to Nikita Pustosviat, a priest who was inflexibly opposed to the reforms of Patriarch Nikon. The priest was known as one of the most uncompromising leaders of the *raskolniks* (dissenters). In 1682 he was executed on Red Square in Moscow.

There are a good many eighteenth-century houses in Suzdal, but they have undergone considerable reconstruction. Much research and restoration is necessary before they can be considered worthy additions to the museum-town.

The tour of Suzdal usually ends at the village of Kideksha where the town's oldest architectural ensemble can be seen to best advantage at sunset.

Prince Yury Dolgoruky, fourth son of Vladimir Monomachus and founder of Moscow, after receiving a principality so far away from Kiev, established himself at Kideksha to await the time when he was to become the ruler of all Russia. Kideksha was near Suzdal, which during that period had not yet developed into a town, but consisted of a number of settlements along the Kamenka River. The Prince chose the site for building his own fortified settlement, because it was a good point for checking traffic (particularly grain shipments) along the Kamenka and Nerl rivers and because it linked Suzdal with other regions in the territory. According to custom the town was built on the high bank and protected by a moat and earth ramparts, the remnants of which still survive.

Inside the low stone wall with a beautiful gateway we see the simple outlines of the Church of St Stephen. West of it there is an early eighteenth-century tent-shaped bell-tower which has a tendency to lean over like the tower of Pisa. The Cathedral of St Boris and St Gleb built in 1152, at the same time as the Transfiguration Cathedral in Pereslavl-Zalessky, stands nearby. It is cruciform in plan, supported by four pillars and crowned by a single dome. The outer walls are divided by flat pilaster strips and sparsely decorated with blind arcading and a band of indented cut stone. The meticulously hewn limestone and the fine seams indicate the hand of experienced stone masons. The craftsmen were probably imported from Galich, which was governed by Yury Dolgoruky's brother. Local workers had not yet acquired such skill.

Kideksha, associated with the martyr princes Boris and Gleb, was considered a shrine and the church built there was consecrated to them. Some experts claim that the figures of two young horsemen depicted in surviving frescoes inside the building are those of Boris and Gleb, the brothers who were later canonized. They became the first Russian saints and for that reason were particularly revered. The sacred nature of this part of the country heightened the importance of Prince Yury's residence.

In 1238, Kideksha was destroyed by the Mongols, but the following year it was rebuilt and the church consecrated anew. Later the Prince's residence was turned into a monastery which functioned until 1764. At that time the monastery's places of worship became ordinary churches for the people of Kideksha which had itself become an ordinary village.

The Cathedral of St Boris and St Gleb suffered considerable damage in the eight hundred years since it was built. Three hundred years ago its vaults and dome caved in. They were repaired with brick, the walls were lowered and covered with a hipped roof. But the cathedral still towers majestically over the river looking out on the lovely expanse of green fields along the Kamenka and Nerl. Only Bogoliubovo has greater appeal than this poetic spot.

71. *Suzdal. Valley of the Kamenka. To the left, the Monastery of St Alexander Nevsky, the Ascension Cathedral and bell-tower. 1695. To the right, walls and towers of the Convent of the Intercession. 16th—18th centuries →*

72. *Suzdal. The kremlin. The Cathedral of the Nativity of the Virgin. 13th–16th centuries*

73. *Suzdal. The kremlin. The Cathedral of the Nativity of the Virgin. Fresco. 13th century*

74. *Suzdal. The kremlin. The Church of St Nicholas from the village of Glotovo. 1766*

75. *Suzdal. The kremlin. The Church of the Transfiguration from the village of Kozliatyevo. 1756*

76. *Suzdal. The Convent of the Deposition of the Robe. 1688. Holy Gates* →

77. *Suzdal. To the left, the Church of St Nicholas. 1720. In the centre, the Cathedral of the Nativity of the Virgin. 13th–16th centuries. To the right, the Cathedral bell-tower. 1635* ⇒

78. *Suzdal. The Convent of the Intercession. The refectory-type Church of the Conception. 1551*

79. *Suzdal. The Church of St Cosmas and St Damian. 1725*

80. *Suzdal. General view of the Convent of the Intercession.*
    16th–18th centuries →

81. *Suzdal. The Kideksha architectural complex.*
    12th–18th centuries ⇒

BOGOLIUBOVO

Meadows covered with succulent grass. Translucent blue shadows in the distance. A small lake, which used to be part of the Nerl River, fringed with reeds and water lilies. And on the grassy knoll an exquisite little church sheltered by tall elms, its outlines reflected in the still water.

There are many fine specimens of old Russian architecture on the Golden Ring. But in the last 800 years none have surpassed the beauty of the Church of the Intercession-on-the-Nerl at the town of Bogoliubovo.

It seems incongruous that this "miracle of poetry in stone" should have been built by the tyrannical Prince Andrei nicknamed "Bogoliubsky" (God-loving) after the village of Bogoliubovo which he had chosen as the site for his fortified castle. The nickname implying a meek and gentle nature was ill-adapted to the proud, arrogant prince, second son of Yury Dolgoruky and a Princess of the Tartar Kipchak tribe. There are a number of references to his military prowess in the chronicles, one of which describes him as "a powerful man and exceedingly brave". Cruel, crafty and far-sighted, Andrei was able to give sound advice to his imperious father after the latter had suffered a temporary reverse in the fight for the Kiev throne: "There's nothing more we can do here, father. Best leave before the cold weather sets in."

When Yury Dolgoruky finally gained his objective and became Grand Prince, he bestowed upon his son the principality of Vyshgorod near Kiev, but the wilful Andrei abandoned it together with his *druzhina* for his beloved Kliazma region where he had lived as a child and whose forests offered reliable protection from the marauding tribes of the steppes. And in leaving the devastated south he had no qualms about taking with him the greatly revered Byzantine icon of the Virgin, the most cherished sacred article in Kievan Rus. Thereafter the icon was known as the *Virgin of Vladimir.*

The region of Vladimir and "the stone city of Bogoliub" (as it is described in the chronicles) belonged to Andrei even in his father's lifetime. After the death of Yury Dolgoruky when Andrei became

Grand Prince, he still did not go "to sit on the throne in Kiev", but made Vladimir the capital of his principality.

At Bogoliubovo on the highest point overlooking the Kliazma River (which has since receded southwards) Andrei built his fortified castle and the Church of the Nativity of the Virgin with arcaded passageways to the residential chambers. There was a spacious courtyard with stone slabs which can still be found some two metres underground. There were quarters for his warriors, stables, and a place for arms and household supplies. The premises were encircled by earth ramparts and a deep moat.

Evidence exists indicating that foreign craftsmen sent by Frederick Barbarossa took part in the construction work. Contacts with western countries were customary. Even during the reign of Yaroslav the Wise, a hundred years before Andrei's time, Kievan Rus ranked with the most powerful countries of Eastern Europe.

The tall towers of the castle commanded a clear view of the surrounding country. Nothing escaped the eye of the watcher – neither mounted messenger, a train of wagons, nor merchant craft sailing along the Nerl towards the Kliazma River. All had to pass by the castle gate, all were stopped and inspected. Merchants had to pay duty on the goods they were carrying. Part of the revenue went to the Prince and part "for the decoration of the House of the Virgin Mary", that is the Church of the Intercession.

The church was built to commemorate the death of Andrei's oldest son who was killed in battle against the Volga Bulgars. It is said that the stone for the construction was brought by the Bulgars as a form of tribute. The building was put up about a mile from the castle on an artificial little island reinforced by a strong foundation right in the delta of the Nerl River.

There must have been adjacent buildings the nature of which we can only surmise, but they have not survived. Even by itself, however, the Church of the Intercession-on-the-Nerl is incredibly beautiful, especially during the spring floods when it appears like a gleaming white vision above the water.

The walls of the small, single-domed cube of the church lean slightly inward, giving the impression of greater height. Everything was done to lead the eye upward, to remind man that there is heaven as well as earth. This upward movement was achieved by the demi-columns, the long narrow windows, the multiple vertical lines of the blind arcading, the slender drum, and the pointed dome.

The carving on the exterior is very fine. The archivolts on the portals seem to be woven of leaves. In the *zakomaras* we see the figure of King David, female masks, doves, griffins and lions. The lion became the emblem of the Vladimir Principality replacing the ger-falcon of Suzdal.

When Russia adopted its religion from Byzantium, it acquired, along with the icons and books, the Greek Church feast days. Many of the holidays, however, did not coincide with the agricultural cycle of this country situated further north. Also, it was desirable for the new Russian capital to establish a holiday of its own. It was probably on the instructions of Andrei Bogoliubsky that the church authorities instituted the festival of the Intercession of the Virgin Mary which had never been an important one in Byzantium. In Russia it soon became very popular because the date, October first according to the old Julian calendar, was so convenient. By that time the harvest was in, the work in the fields completed.

Perhaps the holiday was chosen because a female god had been the principal deity among the Ugro-Finnish tribes of the north-east which had gradually become assimilated with the Russians. New religions, it seems, always retained what was useful from the old.

The female masks on the walls of the Church of the Intercession have broad oriental-type cheek bones. Why? That question is difficult to answer.

What remains of the castle itself is the passageway from the church to the tower with a spiral staircase and a kind of vestibule (*seni*) above it. The architectural décor of the tower repeats the forms of the old Cathedral of the Resurrection (rebuilt in 1751) in the blind arcading, the corner demi-columns with carved capitals, and the *zakomara*, over which a tent-shaped bell-tower was erected later, in the eighteenth century.

The staircase tower witnessed the tragedy that took place on the night of June 29, 1174, the night Prince Andrei was murdered. People closest to him, even his wife, were involved in the plot. The Prince had struggled desperately to escape his assailants, but in vain. After the evil deed was done the murderers broke into the armoury and the treasury. The townspeople joined them in ransacking the palace. The disturbances spread to Vladimir and the whole principality; Andrei's men were robbed and beaten. The Prince's body was "thrown to the dogs", but the court jester who had been devoted to his master risked his life to rescue it, wrap it in a rug and deposit it in the church chapel . . . Later Prince Andrei was canonized by the Church, although he was a cruel man, feared by the boyars and hated by the common people.

True, there was nothing saintly about him. But Andrei Bogoliubsky had the virtue of understanding that the Vladimir-Suzdal region – rich in grain, timber and trade routes – provided a firm foundation for building a state. He chose the rye fields of the Zalesye water-meadows to lay the corner stone of the Great Russia to be. And he left us the finest memorial of medieval Russia, the incomparable Church of the Intercession-on-the-Nerl.

82. *Bogoliubovo. The Church of the Intercession-on-the-Nerl. View from north-west →*

85. *Bogoliubovo. The Church of the Intercession-on-the-Nerl. 1165*

86. *Bogoliubovo. The Church of the Intercession-on-the-Nerl. Blind arcading. 1165*

VLADIMIR

When Kievan Rus was being ravished by hostile nomad tribes, people looked to the north-east for help from Prince Vsevolod. This idea is poignantly expressed in Russia's literary epic *The Lay of Igor's Host:* "Oh, great Prince, if you would only hasten here, albeit in spirit, to watch over your father's throne! You have the power to cleave the waters of the Volga with oars and to bale out the Don with the helmets of your warriors."

In the latter half of the twelfth century a large part of the inhabitants of the Dnieper Basin moved across the Oka River to the Zalesye region where the nucleus of the future Great Russian State was developing, first into the Vladimir-Suzdal principality and later into Muscovy.

The reign of Vsevolod-the-Big-Nest and his older brother Andrei Bogoliubsky marks the height of the power and glory of Vladimir-Suzdal. The fortifications of the new capital Vladimir were as strong, and its churches as beautiful, and sumptuous as those of the old capital city, Kiev.

In 1160, Prince Andrei imported "master craftsmen from all countries" to build the triple-domed Cathedral of the Dormition and to decorate it inside and out with sculpture, frescoes and gilt.

Much of this splendour was destroyed in the fire of 1185. When the cathedral was later restored by Russian stone masons, the chroniclers recorded with great pride that it was no longer necessary to call upon foreign craftsmen.

In the reconstruction the eastern, altar apse was broadened and the other three encased in new walls. The original building was no longer visible, but its *zakomaras* could still be seen above the lower vaulting erected in Vsevolod's time.

The new cathedral was crowned by five large golden domes. The interior, divided into five sections, expanded when big and small arched openings were cut in the old walls.

Some of the original ornamentation is still in evidence – the band of blind arcading with wedge-shaped consoles and carved capitals of Western European type, a line of vertically cut stone above it, and traces of the old frescoes. Vsevolod's craftsmen repeated many of these details on the walls of the new building.

Three hundred years later Aristotle Fioravanti, the Italian architect from Bologna, copied these decorations and used them in the Moscow Kremlin when he was commissioned to build a church patterned on the old ones in Vladimir.

Over the centuries the cathedral was damaged by fire and restored a number of times. But on the whole it preserved its original appearance. A high bell-tower arose next to it in the nineteenth century. It seemed appropriate to the people of that period. But then each generation has its own ideas of beauty.

The twelfth-century icon of *Our Lady of Vladimir*, now in the Tretyakov Gallery (Moscow), used to adorn the Cathedral of the Dormition. It was painted by a highly gifted Byzantine artist.

The cathedral is also famous for the work of Andrei Rublev, the world-renowned icon-painter of medieval Russia. Rublev, Daniil Chorny and their companions' frescoes decorate the two vaults beneath the choir gallery, the pilaster at the left of the altar, and the roundels of broad decorative bands of painted drapery at the bottom of the cathedral walls.

Another superb specimen of architecture in the Vladimir kremlin is the Cathedral of St Demetrius, the court church of Vsevolod III built in 1197. It is a simply designed, single-domed structure typical of the twelfth century, but its harmoniously conceived proportions are imbued with a solemn majesty. At close quarters it impresses one with the wealth of stone carving which cover its walls above the exquisite band of blind arcading.

What a profusion of sculptured decoration – heraldic beasts, birds, foliate patterns, figures of saints, Old Testament kings, prophets, and compositions on mythological, religious and genre themes! King David appears three times in the central *zakomaras.* Alexander the Great is shown being borne to heaven by griffins. A unique "bequest in stone" is the depiction of Prince Vsevolod III enthroned presenting his new-born son to his numerous brothers.

Next to the Church of the Intercession-on-the-Nerl, the Cathedrals of the Dormition and St Demetrius are the finest examples of old Vladimir-Suzdal architecture.

Third in importance among Vladimir's architectural monuments is the main entrance of the town, the Golden Gates dating back to 1164. They are probably the only remaining specimens of such fine quality old Russian military architecture. The sandstone cubic structure pierced with an extremely tall archway was rebuilt in the past century. Circular bastions appeared at the corners and other low buildings at the side. The Gate-church of the Deposition of the Robe was completely reconstructed. With the passage of time the walls of the gates have sunk some five feet into the ground thus detracting from the height of the gateway. In spite of this the Golden Gates built by arrogant Prince Andrei, who, it is said, never bent his head even in church, still looks splendid and formidable.

Vladimir offers several more noteworthy examples of old Russian architecture. The most interesting is the Cathedral of the Dormition at the Princess' Convent founded by Maria, wife of Prince Vsevolod. The cathedral has long served as the burial vault of Grand Princesses. It has been reconstructed again and again, and by studying remaining signs of the work we can trace the development of Russian architecture.

The cathedral is also famous for its magnificent frescoes disposed according to old Russian Church traditions. On the north and south walls we find scenes from the life of the Virgin Mary to whom the church is dedicated. On the piers supporting the vaulting and dome we see bishops and grand princes, the backbone of the militant church. A composition of *The Last Judgement* decorates the west wall. One can well imagine how it must have affected members of the congregation after the service when they filed out by the western doors, how it must have reminded them of the retribution awaiting them.

"Due to the labour and efforts of Vladimir merchants" another Church of the Dormition was built in 1642 on the Kliazma River at the old still extant southern edge of town. The pillars of this lovely little church lift a tight cluster of cupolas and the tent-shaped openwork bell-tower high into the sky.

We gaze with delight at the graceful silhouettes of two eighteenth-century churches of St Nicetas and St Nicholas-on-the-Galleys. At that time the builders still understood that the silhouette was the dominant factor in Russian architecture.

Several buildings of the once wealthy Monastery of the Nativity have also survived. The Warrior-Prince Alexander Nevsky (the Order of Alexander Nevsky still exists in the Soviet Union) was buried at the monastery in 1263. The monastery wall erected on the earth ramparts over a deep moat recalls Vladimir Monomachus, founder of the town of Vladimir. Vladimir Monomachus also built the Yaropolch Fortress (where the town of Viazniki now stands) in memory of his second son Yaropolk. His fourth son Yury (Dolgoruky) laid the corner stone of the Gorokhovets Fortress the same year he founded Moscow. Both towns are situated on the Kliazma River in exceptionally beautiful surroundings. They are off the Golden Ring route, but undoubtedly will be included in another "Ring" covering the south-eastern part of old Muscovy, as our ancestors have left us many fine monuments in that scenic region.

87. *Vladimir. Golden Gates. 1164* →

88. *Vladimir. The Cathedral of the Dormition. 1158–60, 1185–89* →

89, 90. *Vladimir. The Cathedral of the Dormition. Frescoes by Andrei Rublev. 1408*

94. *Vladimir. The Cathedral of the Dormition in the Princess' Convent. Late 15th–early 16th centuries*

95. *Vladimir. The Church of St Nicetas. 1762–65*

There were three Yuryev towns in old Russia. One was in the Kiev Principality, another on Lake Peipus. The third was founded by Prince Yury Dolgoruky in 1152 in the heart of the fertile Suzdal lands north-east of Vladimir, and named after himself. To distinguish it from the others it was called Yuryev-Polsky, that is "Yury's town among the fields".

The sharp-nosed boats carried Yury's warriors up the winding Koloksha River. At the juncture with its tributary, the Gza, Prince Yury ordered his men to build a fortress. According to custom it was surrounded with a moat and earth ramparts, which even with the passage of centuries are still over twenty-two feet high in several places.

No events of great import took place in Yuryev-Polsky. Soon after its establishment it became the capital of Yury's small principality. It witnessed the internecine feuding of his descendants. In the fifteenth century it was handed over to the Lithuanian Prince Svidrigailo as a means of filling his coffers. A century later it was governed by the Tartar Prince Abdul-Latif who had come to Moscow from the Crimea. However, he incurred the displeasure of Ivan III and ended his days in exile at Yuryev-Polsky. Another prince, Kaibulah of Astrakhan, was presented with the town for military services rendered to Ivan the Terrible during the Livonian campaign. Kaibulah adopted Russian ways and prospered. All these temporary rulers did little for the town, being mostly concerned with extorting as much as possible from the inhabitants of the town itself and the outlying villages. Yuriev-Polsky declined. There is little mention of it in the chronicles until the sixteenth century when some progress was noted with the appearance of the first stone buildings at the Monastery of the Archangel Michael founded back in the thirteenth century by Prince Sviatoslav.

A stone wall was built around the monastery in the 1570s. It was reconstructed in the latter half of the seventeenth century except for the west wall. The monastery was approached through the
Holy Gates underneath the five-domed Church of St John the Di-

vine (1670). There were four arched entrances, two for carriages and two for pedestrians, with heavy octagonal columns in between. Above the arcading there is the parvis ornamented with a band of niches and elaborate window surrounds.

The Cathedral of the Archangel Michael is lavishly decorated. Although built one hundered and twenty years after the gateway church, it fits in well with the ensemble, especially with the bell-tower, the monastery's finest feature. The tower's octagonal body rests on a broad, low square base. The surface of the first tier is covered with square niches. The second tier, separated from the first by a line of vertically set stone, is ornamented with three rows of icon recesses. The elaborate cornice above is richly decorated with various carvings and another line of vertically set stone. The arched openings of the bell platform rest on solid demi-columns adorned with bead moulding. The tent-shaped spire pierced with little windows is topped by a shining cupola of glazed green tiles.

Another building that has survived on the monastery premises is the Church of Our Lady of the Sign (1625). It appears to have been reconstructed from an older building. Of particular interest are the single-pillared refectory hall and the small church on the first story.

All the specimens of old Russian architecture stand inside the kremlin earth ramparts which were built in the twelfth century, in Yury Dolgoruky's time. Behind the massive body of an early twentieth-century cathedral rises the town's greatest treasure, the famous Cathedral of St George erected by Prince Sviatoslav in 1234 upon the foundation of an 1152 edifice. After seeing so many sandstone churches on our Golden Ring route, we find the greenish-yellow and silver of the St George walls a delight to the eye. Undoubtedly 740 years ago the limestone was white, and the change in colour is probably due to subsurface water and the lack of insulation between the walls and the foundation. In spring and autumn the lower part of the stone walls acquires a bright-green tinge in spots.

The church was modelled after the very fine Cathedral of St Demetrius in Vladimir. The walls were higher, and topped by pointed *211 zakomaras*. The helmet-shaped dome rested on a graceful elongated drum with narrow windows. With the whole of the exterior covered by magnificent stone carving the building appeared to be encased in lace. Unfortunately, the vaulting and a large part of the walls collapsed in the 1460s as those of the Cathedral of the Nativity in Suzdal had some time earlier. The north wall suffered less than the others, remaining intact up to the band of blind arcading. A section of the west wall has also survived. From them we can judge how fabulously beautiful the church must have been before its collapse and subsequent restoration. We have seen a great deal of fine sculpture on the Golden Ring route, but the carving of the Cathedral of St George is unique. Scenes and individual figures have been executed in high relief and the entire surface of the walls covered with a flat, delicate floral design.

There is reason to believe that the carving was done by two teams of craftsmen, one of them responsible for the figures in high relief, the other for the low decorative background. Some authorities believe that the sculptors may have been Bulgars because of the legend (possibly based on fact) that the sandstone had been brought to Vladimir by Bulgars from the Volga. However, a detailed analysis points to the greater possibility of the work having been executed by craftsmen from Vladimir and Suzdal.

The subject matter is of infinite variety. There is the figure of St George, patron saint of Yury Dolgoruky, heraldic lions with tails in the shape of a strange tree, female masks, a leaping snow leopard, emblem of Vladimir princes, and the fairy-tale Sirin Bird. The craftsmen must have been Russian. Who else would have thought of depicting a centaur dressed in Russian *caftan* and cap! One of the mythical creatures is shown holding a small ax, the other a mace. There is also the figure of a hare. Next to the carving there are four Russian letters thought to be the remains of a signature.

Inside the church looks spacious in spite of its small size. This is probably because the four pillars carrying the vaulting are set wide apart. The impression of size is increased by the chapels and the altar area which is separated from the nave only by a low screen. A small sandstone burial vault adjoins the north-western corner; it contains the tomb of the founder of the church, Grand Prince Sviatoslav, whose life and reign were short but turbulent.

In 1471, the well-known Moscow architect Vasily Yermolin was commissioned to restore the Cathedral of St George. A sad sight greeted him at Yuryev-Polsky. All that remained of the dome and most of the church body was a pile of wreckage. The carved stones which had once been part of harmonious, carefully planned design of high-relief figures and flat floral decoration, had to be sorted and put together again with nothing but guesswork to go by. Many of the carved stones had been smashed beyond repair. Yermolin tried to build a new cathedral more in keeping with the times, but he was not very successful in unifying the multi-figured compositions. He arranged pieces of carving without any kind of order, and used over eighty decorative stones just to put up new vaulting. Other stones found their way into the courtyards of neighbouring houses and into new buildings.

Pieces of the precious carving were later collected and brought inside the church by the archaeologist Piotr Baranovsky. Since the restoration by Yermolin the church has come to be regarded as a kind of stone jigsaw puzzle which many researchers have tried to solve.

96. *Water meadows around Yuryev-Polsky* →

ALEXANDROV

Alexandrova Sloboda, now the town of Alexandrov, is set in pleasant surroundings, the undulating countryside dotted with groves of spruce and birch reminding one of landscapes by the Soviet painter Mikhail Nesterov.

In the centre of town among the low wooden houses we see the spires of old churches rising beyond the white walls and towers of a stone enclosure. This fortress-convent has the dubious distinction of being the only one in medieval Russia to be built with the help of women. The convent was founded here 360 years ago upon a foundation of crumbling palaces built in the time of Ivan the Terrible. Originally the premises were surrounded by an ordinary wooden fence. But when the Elder Cornelius, a hard, ambitious man, became abbot in 1662, a wall and towers of stone were put up by Ivan Gerasimov and his team of stone masons from Moscow.

The Trinity Cathedral, the oldest on the convent grounds, was also partially reconstructed. Built early in the fifteenth century it is a massive rectangular cube with outside walls divided into three parts, each one surmounted by a semicircular recessed arch. A certain resemblance to the older Trinity Cathedral (1422) in Zagorsk led to the belief that the church in Alexandrov had been built one hundred years earlier. But that does not seem possible, since some of the architectural elements are obviously of Italian origin, whereas Italian architects did not appear in Russia until the end of the fifteenth century.

One of the most impressive features of the church is the Golden Gates – massive oak doors covered with copper plates incised with gold. Since the fourteenth century they adorned the Hagia Sophia in Novgorod until Ivan the Terrible brought them to the Sloboda in 1570. In the same year he brought similar doors from Tver after the town had been sacked by his *oprichniki*.

A covered gallery surrounds the cathedral on three sides, and in the crypt several coffins of white limestone are of historical interest.

The Church of the Intercession at the Sloboda used to be Ivan's court chapel. It was reconstructed in the seventeenth century to include the Abbot's Chambers and a refectory. This shut off from view the old tent-shaped roof, which still gives us an idea of the austere beauty of the church as it was 400 years ago. Some of the frescoes have survived.

The Cathedral of the Dormition is supposed to have been built by Vasily III, father of Ivan the Terrible. It too was reconstructed a number of times and little is left of its original appearance.

The Church of the Purification (latter half of the seventeenth century) was erected upon the foundation of an older structure. Two daughters of Tsar Alexei Mikhailovich are buried there.

A prominent part of the Sloboda is the tall tent-shaped bell-tower built on a base of an early sixteenth-century belfry. Strong pillars around the old structure carry the octagon and the gallery with wide arched openings above it. Higher still there are three tiers of arched *kokoshniks* rising toward the faceted tent-shaped roof with the usual narrow windows. Over the roof there is another small octagon with a cupola.

Adjacent to the bell-tower are residential quarters where Marfa, the step-sister of Peter the Great, lived in exile from 1698 to 1707 after her brother had forced her to take the veil. The woman who later bacame Empress Elizabeth of Russia had also been banished to Alexandrova Sloboda for nine years.

The dark period of the Sloboda's history is connected with Tsar Ivan the Terrible. For seventeen years the Sloboda had been his residence. It was from there that Ivan proclaimed the establishment of his select, terror-inspiring corps, the *oprichniki*, and penned his scathing epistles to Prince Kurbsky who had enraged him by escaping execution. It was there that Ivan signed the harsh conditions of the truce with Poland and Sweden after losing the long war with Livonia and forfeiting the gains of his father and grandfather. And it was from there that he led his army of *oprichniki* and landed gentry to strike at the big trade centres of Novgorod and Tver, and to swoop down upon the estates of unruly boyars. Not long before his death Tsar Ivan left the Sloboda for Moscow.

104. *Alexandrov. The Church of the Intercession. 16th century.*
The Refectory and bell-tower. 17th century

ZAGORSK

The Museum Zone at Zagorsk was established under a decree of Lenin in 1920. No wonder it is known as "a jewel among jewels" incorporating as it does a splendid architectural ensemble, as well as magnificent art collections including old Russian painting and the treasures in the vaults of the former Trinity-Sergius Monastery. The monastery at Zagorsk was also a fortress, notable for having once withstood a 16-month siege.

Three hundred and sixty years ago Polish invading forces plunged the territory of old Russia in a sea of fire. All the towns suffered. Wall towers collapsed in crimson clouds of smoke, blood ran along the streets. The Fortress of the Trinity Monastery alone stood firm, like a little island in the inundated land. It was heroically defended mainly by the peasants of nearby villages against invading armies ten and even twenty times their own number. The whole country realized that if the monastery fell, it meant the end of Rus.

And the nation won. The armies of the arrogant Polish leader Hetman Sapieha retreated in disgrace from the monastery grounds. The little fortress of Zagorsk thus became the forerunner of the heroic towns of the Great Patriotic War (1941–45).

The low walls of the monastery, erected in 1540–50, were patterned after those of Kitai-Gorod (a district in old Moscow). After the memorable siege they were made higher. The towers which had sustained the most damage were rebuilt. Today there are eleven towers, two of them with entrance gates. Three of the four circular corner towers have retained their original appearance to a greater degree than the others. They are the Piatnitskaya, Vodianaya, and Plotnichya towers. The fourth, Utichya Tower, was later topped by an ornamental stone steeple in the "Naryshkin" baroque style. At the beginning of the last century an addition was built on to the Red Tower with the Holy Gates.

Inside the monastery walls we see the very old cathedral, its roof and dome shining with gold. The cathedral was erected in 1422, the year its founder, Sergius of Radonezh, was canonized and formally proclaimed "patron of the Russian land".

Sergius (Bartholomew before taking his vows) was born of a Rostov boyar family of modest means. His father had been granted the little town of Radonezh as a kind of "living" by the Grand Prince of Muscovy. Sergius was known as a political as well as a religious figure. He strove to unify the Russian lands and to rally support for the fight against the Mongols. The Russian People's Volunteers, which in 1380 routed Khan Mamai, gathered at the walls of the Trinity Monastery. Sergius not only inspired the armies of Moscow, but also persuaded other appanaged princes to join the ranks of Prince Dmitry Donskoi.

The relics of Sergius are buried at the Trinity Cathedral and the pall with his image is at the Zagorsk Museum. Sergius was tall, broad-shouldered and had a thick head of hair even as an old man.

The iconostasis of the cathedral contains paintings by Andrei Rublev and his team, among them a copy of his world-famous *Old Testament Trinity*. The original is kept at the Tretyakov Gallery in Moscow.

The Church of the Holy Ghost was already built of brick in 1476 by stone masons from Pskov. It is an unusual type of ecclesiastical building with the bell-tower under the dome.

The construction of the monastery's cathedral, the large, five-domed Cathedral of the Dormition, was begun in 1559 during the reign of Ivan the Terrible. It was completed twenty-five years later under Tsar Fiodor Ioannovich. The severe, simple lines of the building give it a majestic appearance. Inside there is a huge, carved iconostasis with high platforms for the choir on the reverse side. The voices of the monks, people used to say, floated down from there as though from heaven. The work of the icon-painter Simon Ushakov can be seen on the iconostasis. Hammered copper chandeliers of exquisite workmanship hang from the dome. The walls and vaulting are decorated with frescoes, which were painted in the summer of 1684 by a team of 35 artists headed by Dmitry Grigoryev. The names of the painters are inscribed on the west wall under broad decorative bands of painted drapery with a pattern of roundels.

The low, simply designed, rectangular structure at the northwest corner of the Cathedral of the Dormition is the burial vault of the Godunov family.

Tsar Boris was not remembered kindly, nor was his wife, the daughter of cruel Maliuta Skuratov, head of the *oprichniki* during the reign of Ivan the Terrible. Tsar Boris's son was a neutral character, soon forgotten. Princess Xenia alone was remembered with gratitude. A woman of rare beauty, sympathy and goodness, she was also an excellent embroiderer at a time when the art of embroidery was highly valued. An altar-cloth "The Queen did stand. . . " made by Xenia Godunova in 1610 is on exhibit at the Museum. It shows the Virgin Mary, Christ, and St John the Baptist with St Sergius of Radonezh and Nikon in attitudes of devotion. The work delicately done on velvet in silk, gold and silver thread and precious stones is a work of art.

The assassins who killed Xenia's mother and brother had spared her life to hand her over to Dmitry the Pretender. But soon she was banished to a distant convent and later transferred to another one. Her life as Sister Olga (after taking the veil) was filled with grief, misfortune and suffering, which she bore stoically. Tales of her saintly character and tragic destiny have come down to us in song and legend, and have also been recorded in the chronicles with warmth and sympathy. People loved and pitied her believing that she suffered for the sins of her father.

As though to distract attention from the gloomy vault, the cheerful-looking Chapel-over-the-Well (late seventeenth century) stands on the other side of the cathedral's western façade. The architecture is in the typical "Naryshkin" style – the usual basic cube carrying three octagons. Another Chapel-over-the-Well (also late seventeenth century) stands on the other side of the monastery wall, on the river bank, east of the Church of the Presentation in the Temple and the Church of St Paraskeva Piatnitsa, both built in 1547.

The Chapel, known as the Piatnitskaya because of its proximity to the church, has lost many of its decorative elements and has sunk into the ground, but the undulating roof with the two apertured octagons, the fine carving on the entrance portal, and traces of the surrounds indicate that this little structure must have been lovely indeed.

Late in the seventeenth century it was decided to reconstruct the three hundred-year-old refectory. The work was done from 1686 to 1692. Today we see the building set up on a high basement with an open gallery and a wide staircase. It is decorated with carved demi-columns, semicircular shell-gables, and window surrounds of stylized vine-leaf design. The walls are painted in a checker-board design of red, yellow, blue and green. Inside, the huge hall is covered by tunnel-vault roofing built according to the most advanced methods of the time. The painting on the walls and vaulting is late nineteenth century, but for that period it is interesting. The church at the end of the hall and separated from it by a gilt hammered-metal railing is remarkable for its beautiful carved iconostasis and the floor laid with blocks of reddish-brown jasper.

An impressive example of early seventeenth-century architecture is the building of the Infirmary with the attached Church of St Zosimus and St Sabas, the only tent-roofed church in the monastery ensemble. Not so long ago the church, practically hidden by the superstructure of an ordinary building, was gradually deteriorating. It was restored to its original appearance by the gifted architect I. Trofimov, who had long been doing reconstruction work at the monastery. Now the beautiful red and white building with its tall, faceted, tent-shaped roof is one of the most picturesque sites on the monastery grounds.

The Gate-church of St John the Baptist was built in 1693–99 by the Stroganovs, a distinguished family of merchants and manufacturers. Although the church has lost four of its five domes, it is still a wonderful monument of the past with a décor similar to that of the Refectory.

The spacious "Chertogi" Palace, stopover residence of Tsar Alexei Mikhailovich, also is from the second half of the seventeenth century. The Tsar often visited the Trinity-Sergius Monastery, which was considered the most revered shrine in the State of Muscovy. Since a retinue of some 500 people accompanied the Tsar, the royal residence had to be large to accommodate all of them. Simple in its outlines, the building was once richly ornamented with tiles, fragments of which still remain. The sculptural decoration and two tiled stoves lend interest to the interior.

An unusual "monument of three centuries" is the elaborate Metropolitan's Residence. From the main northern façade it appears to have two stories. However, a closer look from the north reveals a lower story which was cut into the slope of the hill in the sixteenth century. The floor above it was added in the seventeenth, while a second story went up in the mid-eighteenth when the entire building was decorated and the Trinity-Sergius architectural complex was in the last stage of construction.

The little Church of St Micah was built during the same period. It seems to have been put next to the sumptuous Refectory for contrast. But this unusual though modest church is interesting in itself. Even a structure of secondary importance can be attractive if the architect is a gifted one.

The main entrance to the monastery was through the Pilgrim Tower gate on the north side of the wall. The old buildings which stood opposite the Pilgrim Tower were damaged by fire and were dismantled in 1745 in order to direct the stream of pilgrims toward the Cathedral of the Dormition and from there to the tomb of St Sergius in the Trinity Cathedral. At about the same time construction started on the Church of Our Lady of Smolensk according to a plan drawn up by Dmitry Ukhtomsky. Later he established Russia's first school for architects, which produced outstanding designers such as Kazakov and Blank, assistant to the famous Rastrelli.

The Church of Our Lady of Smolensk (Hodigitria) was one of Ukhtomsky's early projects. It is a graceful building of unusual architectural forms, decorated in the "Elizabethan" baroque fashion. An octagon with alternating concave and convex walls, it rests on a high sandstone socle and has four open porches (three of them have been restored). Wide staircases with carved balustrades lead up to them and to the three doors and altar alcove. Each door is decorated with similar portals and flanked by paired columns. An octagonal dome supports the elegant lantern with narrow arched windows. Surmounting the entire structure is a helmet-shaped cupola topped by a cross over a crescent symbolizing the Christians' victory over Moslem Turkey.

The Church of Our Lady of Smolensk was greatly distorted by additions and reconstructions of every kind. For a long time we didn't know the name of its creator. Its construction, according to legend, was connected with the secret marriage of Empress Elizabeth to Alexei Razumovsky, a member of the court choir. It was said that Rastrelli designed the building. But the efforts of the architect Komarov not only restored to the monastery one of its most beautiful components but also established that the architect was Dmitry Ukhtomsky, the last and most gifted of the architects who worked on the ensemble of the Trinity-Sergius Monastery.

It was Ukhtomsky who put the finishing touch to the ensemble by conceiving the majestic five-tiered bell-tower which unifies the entire complex of buildings at Zagorsk.

In taking our leave, we once more catch sight of the golden crown of the Trinity-Sergius Monastery, its bell-tower, a priceless relic of old Russian architecture, which we are sure not to forget for many years to come.

105. *Zagorsk. The Trinity-Sergius Monastery. View from south →*

106. *Zagorsk. The Trinity-Sergius Monastery. To the left, the Trinity Cathedral. 1422. To the right, the Church of the Holy Ghost. 1476 ⇒*

107. *Zagorsk. The Trinity-Sergius Monastery. The Trinity Cathedral (1422) with the Chapel of St Nikon (1548–1623)*

108. *Zagorsk. The Trinity-Sergius Monastery. The Cathedral of the Dormition. 1559–85*

112. *Zagorsk. The Trinity-Sergius Monastery. Predtechensky building. 17th century*

LIST OF ILLUSTRATIONS

ЗОЛОТОЕ КОЛЬЦО

Альбом (на английском языке)

Издание четвертое

Издательство „Аврора". Ленинград. 1988

Изд. № 2158. (6-00)

Отпечатано при посредничестве
Внешторгиздата

Printed and bound in Yugoslavia